Members of the Monopolies and 1

Sir Godfray Le Quesne QC* (*Chairman*)
Mr J D Eccles (*Deputy Chairman*)
Sir Alan Neale KCB MBE (*Deputy Chairman*)
Mr J G Ackers
Professor A D Bain*†
Mr M B Bunting
Mr P H Dean
Professor K D George
Mr H L G Gibson OBE*
Mr P Goldman CBE
Professor R M Goode OBE
Mr D G Goyder
Mr E A B Hammond OBE
Mr H H Hunt
Mr L Kelly
Mr M S Lipworth
Mr S R Lyons
Dr R L Marshall OBE*‡
Mrs C M Miles*
Mr L Mills
Mr B C Owens
Mr D G Richards
Mr J S Sadler CBE*
Mr N L Salmon
Mr R G Smethurst
Sir Ronald Swayne MC
Mr J J Wallis
Mr N E D Burton (*Secretary*)

---

*These members formed the group which was responsible for this report.
†Professor Bain resigned on 31 December 1982.
‡Since the Report was signed, Dr Marshall has ceased to be a member of the Commission on the expiry of his term of appointment.

Contents

The location of the coalfields of Great Britain

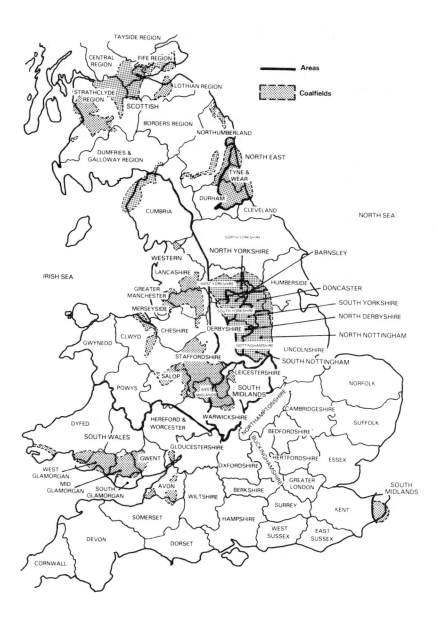

Parliamentary Statement by the Secretary of State for Energy on 19 February 1981

As the House knows, there was a tripartite meeting of the coal industry yesterday. This had been called at the industry's request to discuss the situation which had arisen following the meeting in London on 10 February between the NCB and the unions. At that meeting the NCB had outlined its approach to the current problems facing the industry. It had put forward a four-point plan for bringing the supply and demand for coal back into balance, whilst maintaining investment for the future. The plan included an accelerated programme for the closure of older capacity approaching the end of its productive life. This was to be discussed in detail in the areas. The Board believed its plan to be reasonable and acceptable. However, fears and anxiety among the work force arose through rumoured and distorted impressions of what was being proposed.

It was against this background that yesterday's meeting took place. At the meeting three main points were raised—closures, financial constraints and coal imports. I said that the Government were prepared to discuss the financial constraints with an open mind and also with a view to movement. The chairman of the National Coal Board said that in the light of this the Board would withdraw its closure proposals and re-examine the position in consultation with the unions. I accordingly invited the industry to come forward with new proposals consistent with 'Plan for Coal'.

As regards imports, I pointed out that these would, in any case, fall this year from their 1980 levels. The industry representatives said that they wished to see this figure brought down to its irreducible minimum. I said that the Government would be prepared to look, with a view to movement, at what could be done to go in this direction.

I welcome the decision of the national executive committee of the NUM today and hope that its lead will be followed. I will be meeting the industry again next Wednesday.

Source: Hansard 19 February 1981.

APPENDIX 2.3
(referred to in paragraph 2.33)

Longwall mining

1. Since nationalisation, most deep-mined coal in the United Kingdom has been obtained by longwall methods, so called because the coal is removed in one operation by means of a long working face or 'wall'. There are several ways in which the longwall system can be operated; principally by advance mining and retreat mining or a combination of these.

2. Figure 1 shows a simplified plan of a mine worked by advance mining methods. Two parallel tunnels or roadways are driven through the coal seam generally between 200 and 300 metres apart. (This distance effectively determines the length of the working face which varies according to geological conditions and other technical factors.) These two roadways are joined by a drivage in the seam at right-angles to them and this forms the working face. The two roadways are usually supported by steel arched roof supports and the roof of the working face is supported by hydraulically powered roof supports. The operation of the powered supports is described in paragraph 5.

3. The coal is cut by a cutter-loader machine which travels up and down the coal face. In systems most popular in the United Kingdom the machine travels on top of the armoured face conveyor (AFC). (The AFC is described in paragraph 4.) Typically, the cutting element of the machine consists of a rotating drum fitted with picks (although there are other methods). As the machine moves along the coal face it cuts into the coal which is then pushed backwards on to the AFC. At each pass the machine cuts coal off the face to a depth of up to one metre and the face can advance at speeds in excess of 25 metres per week.

4. The AFC, which runs the whole length of the face, consists of a steel trough built in sections. Steel flights within the trough, which are pulled by endless chains, drag the coal along the AFC to the end of the coal face where it is taken away by other conveyors. The AFC is built in sections so that it can be pushed forward and snaked round behind the cutter-loader as it moves along the face. A detailed diagram of the AFC is at Figure 2.

5. The advance of the coal cutter is such that a large area of roof is rapidly left behind which is in need of prompt support to avoid collapse. This rapid support is achieved by means of the hydraulically powered roof supports. Their operation is illustrated in Figures 3(*a*) to 3(*d*). The basic support position as the cutter-loader passes is as in Figure 3(*a*) with the vertical rams extending to bring the upper beam into contact with the roof. After the cutter-loader has passed, the horizontal ram is extended to push the AFC forward to the newly exposed coal face (Figure 3(*b*)). The vertical rams are then lowered so that the upper beam drops sufficiently for the horizontal ram to be retracted, thus pulling the powered support forward to the AFC (Figure 3(*c*) and 3(*d*)). The vertical rams are then extended once more to bring the upper beam into contact with and to support the roof as in Figure

3(*a*). This whole process is repeated along the face as the cutter-loader passes. The roof area behind the powered supports, except for the packing at the side of the roads, is left unsupported and allowed to collapse.

6. When the face is being worked in advance, the access roads at either end must move at the same rate as the face. This is made difficult by the amount of machinery that it is necessary to have there; the conveyors for taking away the coal, the motors to drive the AFC, the hydraulic tank pump and motor for the powered supports, the electrical supply switchgear, and the ripping machines to advance the roadway. With retreat mining the two access roads are driven the full length of the panel of coal to be extracted. The coal is then obtained by working the face backwards along the roadways. Figure 4 shows a simplified plan of the method. Another advantage of this method is that it provides almost complete information about the coal that is to be worked, giving early warning of faults or other difficult mining conditions. The disadvantages are that it involves high investment costs and there is a delay before coal is produced so that financing charges are high. The method is not always applicable because of adverse mining conditions, for instance, where strata pressures are very high, maintaining the access roads might entail an unacceptable level of repair work. These problems can only be overcome in the particular conditions which permit retreat working. Where this method of mining has been possible the output per day is significantly higher than it is for advancing faces.

Figure 1

A simplified plan of advance mining

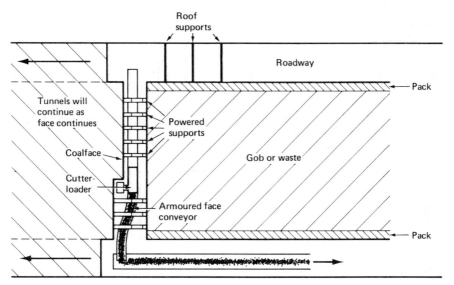

Source: MMC.

Figure 2

Detail of an armoured face conveyor (AFC)

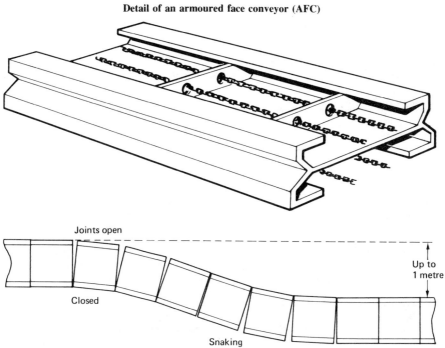

Source: MMC.

FIGURE 3

The operation of hydraulically powered roof supports

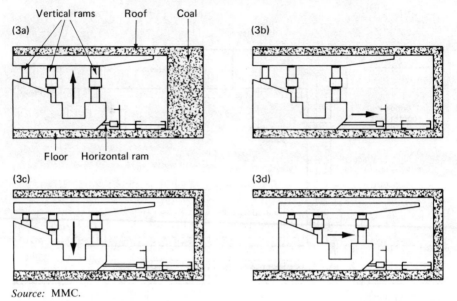

Source: MMC.

FIGURE 4

A simplified plan of retreat mining

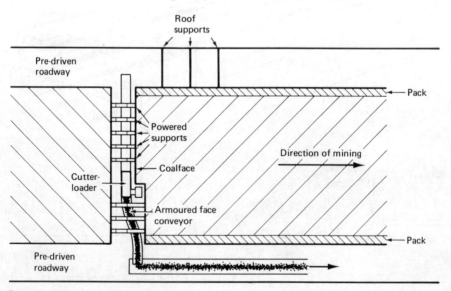

Source: MMC.

Opencast mining operations

1. Before mining can begin certain preliminary works must be completed. Access roads, site offices, workshops and car parks are constructed. The entire site is securely fenced against stock, and surface water drainage ditches and lagoons are excavated to control run-off from the site and prevent the pollution of rivers and watercourses outside the site boundary. Provision is made for diverting public utility services which will be affected by the working of the site, together with footpaths and roads. Wheel washing plant is provided to prevent mud and slurry being deposited on public roads.

2. Mining operations begin with the stripping and storage of topsoil from the operational area and those areas to be used for buildings, plant yards, subsoil and overburden dumps and access roads. On small sites all the soil stripping may be done at the same time but on larger sites stripping will be progressive in advance of coaling operations. The thickness of topsoil to be stripped, specified in the Authorisation, averages at least 0·3m but on some sites the amount available will be less than this and care must be taken to avoid loss or wastage during stripping. Sufficient subsoil is also stripped and stored to enable a layer of at least 0·6m thickness to be laid as a cushion between the topsoil and overburden at the restoration stage. Coaling contracts stipulate that if sufficient soil is not available, any suitable soil-making material found during the course of excavation will be saved and stored by the contractor to make up the required quantities.

3. Stripping and stacking of both topsoil and subsoil is normally carried out by scrapers, which may be self-propelled or tractor-drawn. This operation can only be carried out when ground conditions are suitably dry. Topsoil and subsoil mounds are normally located close to the perimeter of the site, to act as baffles against noise from the site and as visual screens. These mounds are grassed and kept weed-free by periodic maintenance. No heavy machinery is allowed to run over them until they are lifted for re-spreading.

4. With the topsoil and subsoil stripped from the working areas the contractor is free to commence the removal of the overburden and win the coal. His choice of main excavating plant and method of working is largely dictated by the geology of the site and by other factors such as plant availability, cost, his expertise and environmental considerations. No two sites are alike so only a generalised outline of the working methods can be given.

5. The most common method, on sites with seams dipping at a shallow angle of less than 1 in 10, is to open an initial cut along the outcrop of the seam. If the seam does not outcrop within the excavation boundary a box cut is taken. Work then proceeds by taking successive parallel cuts with the overburden from each new cut being cast or transported into the void of

the previous coaled-out cut, to minimise the amount of rehandling of material that is required. The final void is filled with the spoil from the initial cut and other overburden material accumulated above ground. The back-filled overburden is progressively levelled by dozers and graders to the required contours. Other general methods of working include:

(a) dip cuts—cuts parallel to the dip of the seam, advancing across the strike;

(b) diagonal cuts—cuts advancing obliquely across the strike; and

(c) strike cuts—cuts starting from the deepest part of the seam and advancing up-dip; sometimes called retreat working.

6. The overburden is removed by dragline or excavators to within a few centimetres of the top of the coal seam. (See Figures 1 to 4.) To ensure that minimal contamination of the coal occurs the remaining overburden is removed by smaller plant or hand labour. When the top of the coal seam has been cleaned the coal is dug mechanically, taking care to avoid contamination from the strata below the coal seam. Leaves of coal separated by more than a 25mm dirt band are considered to be separate seams and are lifted independently. Seams down to 130mm thickness are commonly recovered cleanly and economically. The only treatment necessary for the majority of opencast coal is crushing and dry screening to the required size.

Environmental controls

7. In order to minimise the impact of opencast mining on the environment, certain mandatory constraints (including those specified in the Authorisation) are written into contract documents. The Executive's Site Engineer supervises all site operations throughout the contract period, with special attention to the enforcement of these constraints. A liaison committee is formed for each site, including representatives from local planning authorities, local residents and other parties with interests in the site so that environmental problems can be speedily resolved.

8. The major aspects which are the subject of specific supervision are as follows:

(a) *Noise:* Most sites have maximum permitted noise levels for day and night working and these restrict operations. Noise levels on all sites are regularly monitored.

(b) *Dust:* Water bowsers are used to spray the site roads so as to suppress dust.

(c) *Blasting:* Permitted blasting limits are imposed on all sites in order to prevent damage to structures outside the boundary of the site and monitoring of blasting vibrations is undertaken on all production sites on a regular basis.

(d) *Water pollution:* Settling lagoons are constructed on every site to improve the quality of effluent leaving the site. Flocculating agents are often used to assist in this process.

(e) *Visual aspect:* Baffle embankments are erected parallel to the site boundary to screen the workings from view from outside the site. Spoil mounds are constructed within specified heights to reduce their visual impact.

These environmental constraints affect the method of working and result in increased costs of operating and of supervision by the Executive. In addition, the Executive has, over the past five years, sponsored several research projects of a long-term nature which include research in the field of noise, dust, blasting, water and slope stability.

Land restoration and rehabilitation

9. Following the coaling operations the overburden is graded to previously agreed contours. All levelling and final grading is carefully done so as to avoid compaction and to ensure that, when the subsoil and topsoil are replaced and after allowing for subsequent settlement, the site will blend with the surrounding contours and the restored land can be adequately drained. Alternative land forms can be provided to meet the requirements of the local planning authorities. A formal restoration meeting is held on site between the Executive, the Ministry of Agriculture, Fisheries and Food (DAFF in Scotland, WOAD in Wales), the local planning authority and any land owners or occupiers to confirm the agreement of all parties to the final land form. Providing the contours are judged to be satisfactory, the replacement of subsoil and topsoil can proceed.

10. Before the subsoil is replaced, the overburden is scarified with a rooter or a winged subsoiler to a depth of at least 300mm. This breaks up any surface panning caused by the passage of vehicles during backfilling operations and enables any large stones or other extraneous material to be removed. Subsoil mounds are then lifted and re-spread using scrapers, in two separate layers about 0·3m deep. Each layer is thoroughly rooted to remove compaction and stones or any other objects which may interfere with drainage or farming equipment. Watercourses are re-established, diversions and lagoons filled in, access roads broken up and office and plant yard areas cleared. Finally, the topsoil is re-spread by scraper and is cultivated to loosen the surface and to provide an acceptable seed bed which is seeded to grass as soon as practical as a preliminary to the rehabilitation process.

11. With topsoiling satisfactorily completed, the contractual restoration by the site contractor is complete and the site is accepted by the Ministry of Agriculture, Fisheries and Food (DAFF in Scotland, WOAD in Wales), to commence the following rehabilitation work over a five year minimum period, during which time these bodies act as agents for the Executive.

   (a) The reinstatement, when necessary, of the fixed farm features, such as fences, ditches, hedges, trees and woodlands. This is the responsibility of the Executive, although the actual work is carried out by specialist contractors.

   (b) The rehabilitation of the land by careful management of cultivations, manuring, cropping, control of grazing and the design and installation of a permanent under-drainage system and the provision of water to the fields. Wherever practicable, the owners and former occupiers of the land are employed to carry out the actual operations, otherwise the work is done by agricultural contractors or by MAFF, DAFF or WOAD staff.

12. The agency is terminated upon completion of rehabilitation. Land owned by the Executive is normally transferred to Coal Industry Estates Limited (see Chapter 17) for eventual sale but occasionally may be disposed of direct to a local authority as part of an exchange relating to the land requirements for a new site. Land not owned by the Executive is returned to its owner(s) or former tenants and the Executive's rights of occupancy are terminated.

FIGURE 1

Diagrammatic view of multiple-seam mining operation

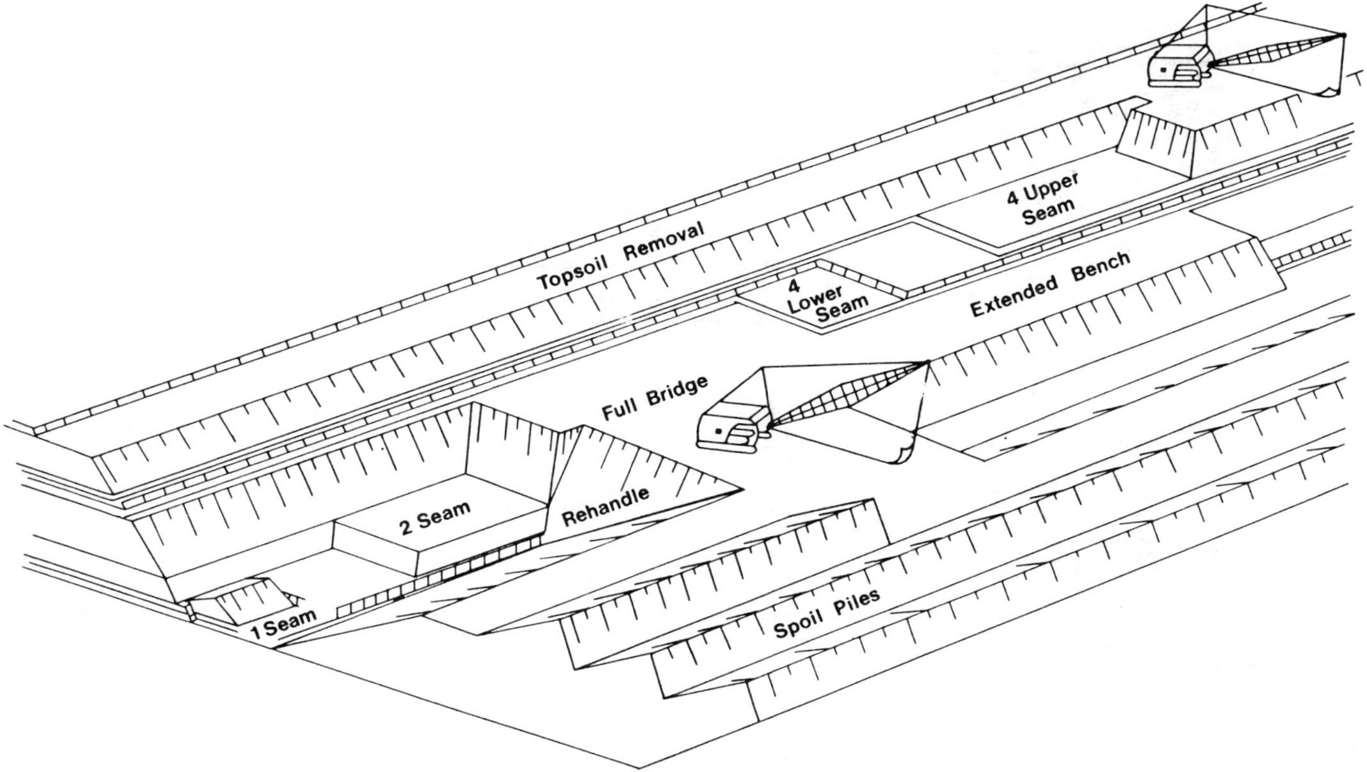

Topsoil Removal

4 Upper Seam

4 Lower Seam

Extended Bench

Full Bridge

Rehandle

2 Seam

1 Seam

Spoil Piles

Source: The NCB.

11

FIGURE 2

Dragline operations A and B

(A) Muck "A" being handled by Dragline as a chop down operation from high wall.

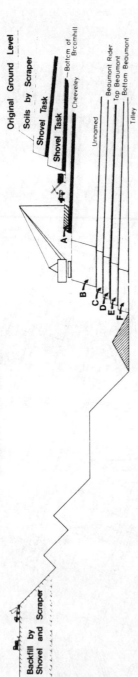

(B) Muck "B" handled as a line dig and cast by Dragline on high wall.

Spoil levelled out by Dozer on low wall to form Dragline bench.

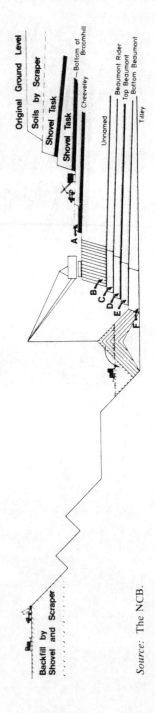

Source: The NCB.

12

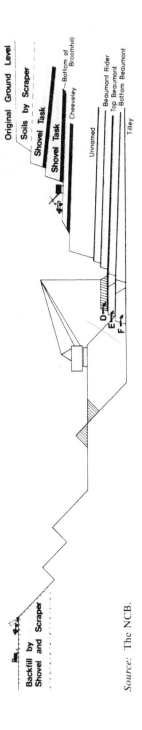

FIGURE 3

Dragline operations C and D

(C) Muck "C" handled by Backacter and Truck.

(D) Muck "D" handled by Dragline from low wall after taking pilot cut by Backacter.

Source: The NCB.

13

FIGURE 4

Dragline operations E and F

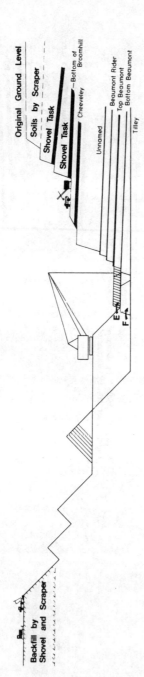

(E) Muck "E" moved by Dragline from low wall in chopping operation.

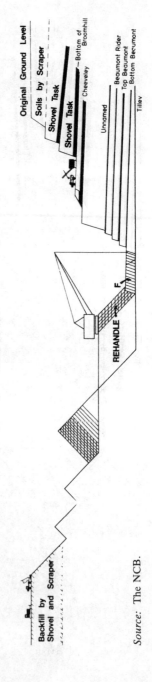

(F) Muck "F" and Rehandled Material moved clear of Bottom Seam by Dragline from low wall.

Source: The NCB.

14

Organisation of the National Coal Board

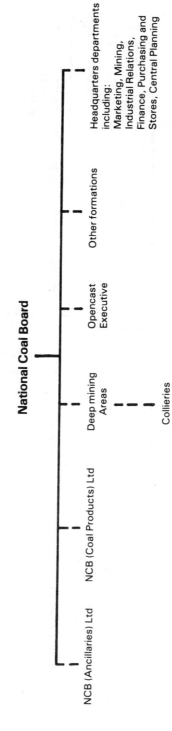

National Coal Board

NCB (Ancillaries) Ltd

NCB (Coal Products) Ltd

Deep mining Areas

Collieries

Opencast Executive

Other formations

Headquarters departments including:
Marketing, Mining, Industrial Relations, Finance, Purchasing and Stores, Central Planning

Source: The NCB.

The Opencast Executive (I)

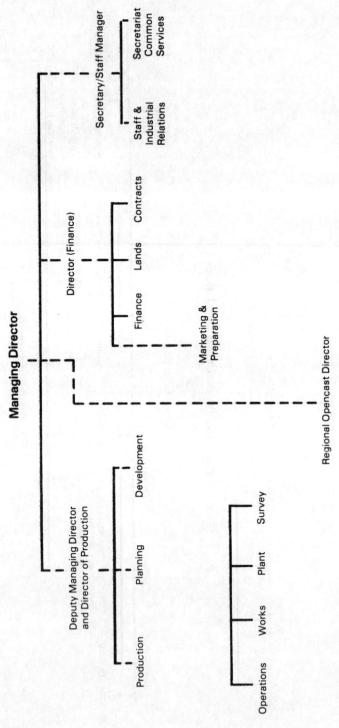

Source: The NCB.

The Opencast Executive (II)

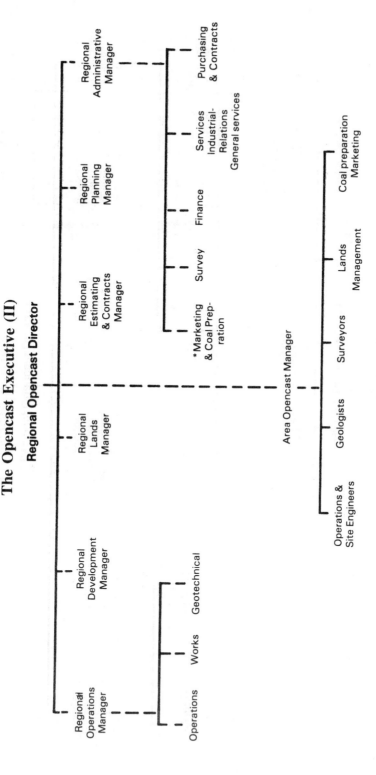

Regional Opencast Director

Regional Operations Manager

Regional Development Manager

Regional Lands Manager

Regional Estimating & Contracts Manager

Regional Planning Manager

Regional Administrative Manager

Operations

Works

Geotechnical

*Marketing & Coal Preparation

Survey

Finance

Services
Industrial-Relations
General services

Purchasing & Contracts

Area Opencast Manager

Operations & Site Engineers

Geologists

Surveyors

Lands Management

Coal preparation Marketing

*In some regions, responsibility for the branch lies with the Regional Operations Manager.

Source: The NCB.

17

Headquarters Mining Department

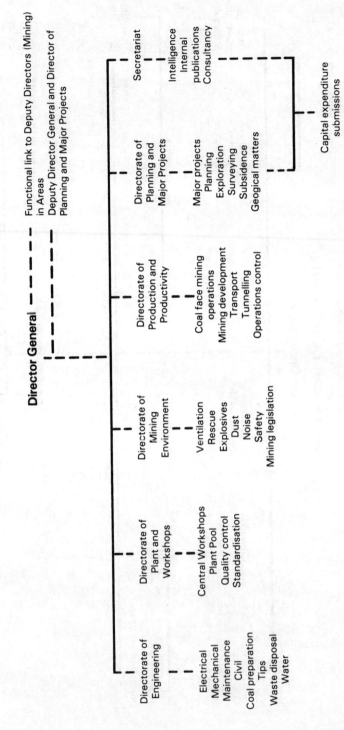

Director General

Functional link to Deputy Directors (Mining) in Areas
Deputy Director General and Director of Planning and Major Projects

Directorate of Engineering
- Electrical
- Mechanical
- Maintenance
- Civil
- Coal preparation
- Tips
- Waste disposal
- Water

Directorate of Plant and Workshops
- Central Workshops
- Plant Pool
- Quality control
- Standardisation

Directorate of Mining Environment
- Ventilation
- Rescue
- Explosives
- Dust
- Noise
- Safety
- Mining legislation

Directorate of Production and Productivity
- Coal face mining operations
- Mining development
- Transport
- Tunnelling
- Operations control

Directorate of Planning and Major Projects
- Major projects
- Planning
- Exploration
- Surveying
- Subsidence
- Geological matters

Secretariat
- Intelligence
- Internal publications
- Consultancy

Capital expenditure submissions

Source: The NCB.

18

Marketing Department

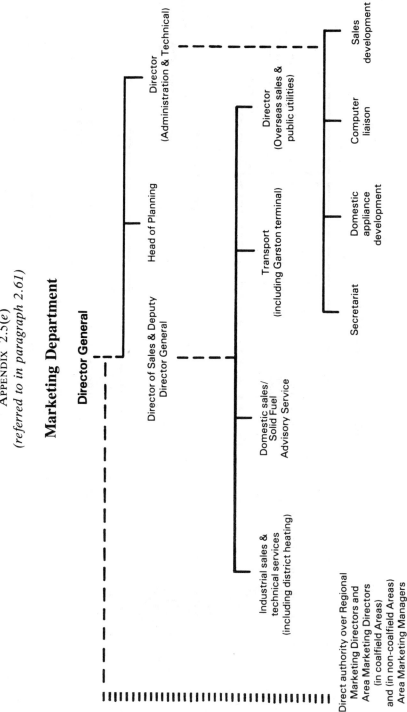

Director General

Director of Sales & Deputy Director General

Head of Planning

Director (Administration & Technical)

Director (Overseas sales & public utilities)

Industrial sales & technical services (including district heating)

Domestic sales/ Solid Fuel Advisory Service

Transport (including Garston terminal)

Secretariat

Domestic appliance development

Computer liaison

Sales development

Direct authority over Regional Marketing Directors and Area Marketing Directors (in coalfield Areas) and (in non-coalfield Areas) Area Marketing Managers

Source: The NCB.

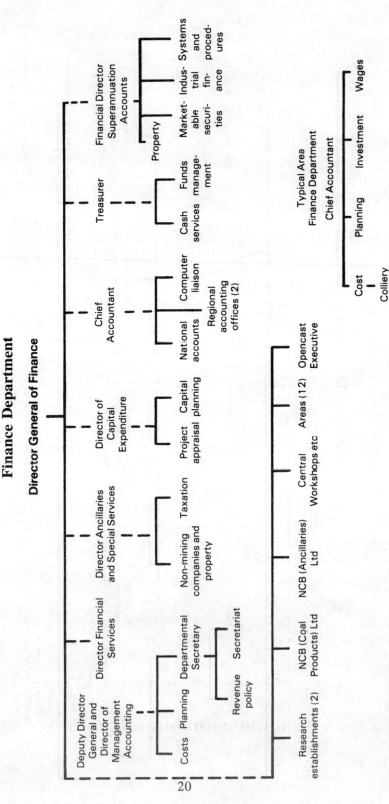

APPENDIX 2.5(f)
(referred to in paragraph 2.61)

Finance Department

Director General of Finance

Deputy Director General and Director of Management Accounting

Director Financial Services

Director Ancillaries and Special Services

Director of Capital Expenditure

Chief Accountant

Treasurer

Financial Director Superannuation Accounts

Costs
Planning

Departmental Secretary

Revenue policy

Secretariat

Non-mining companies and property

Taxation

Project appraisal

Capital planning

National accounts

Computer liaison

Regional accounting offices (2)

Cash services

Funds management

Property

Market-able securities

Indus-trial fin-ance

Systems and proced-ures

Research establishments (2)

NCB (Coal Products) Ltd

NCB (Ancillaries) Ltd

Central Workshops etc

Areas (12)

Opencast Executive

Typical Area Finance Department
Chief Accountant

Cost

Planning

Investment

Wages

Colliery cost clerks

Source: The NCB.

National Coal Board Industrial Relations Department as at December 1981

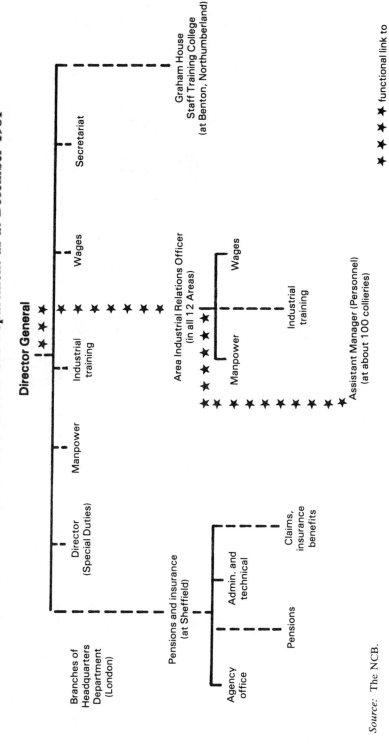

Source: The NCB.

(referred to in paragraph 3.2)

National Coal Board and subsidiaries: summary of financial results 1972–73 to 1981–82

£ million

Year ended March	1972–73	1973–74	1974–75	1975–76	1976–77	1977–78	1978–79	1979–80	1980–81	1981–82
Turnover	1,033·1	913·6	1,589·6	1,982·2	2,426·6	2,733·1	2,989·4	3,740·4	4,186·5	4,727·5
Trading results—profit/(loss)										
Mining activities										
Deep mines	(59·9)	(135·7)	(35·7)	(31·1)	31·9	0·3	(26·1)	(121·4)	(106·5)	(226·1)
Opencast	19·4	15·8	46·8	63·1	65·4	88·1	97·6	109·7	156·9	156·9
Other	4·7	3·8	2·2	3·7	3·8	4·5	6·2	5·5	11·5	21·0
Total mining activities	(35·8)	(116·1)	13·3	35·7	101·1	92·9	77·7	(6·2)	61·9	(48·2)
Other activities*	9·9	14·6	30·3	21·6	15·4	15·1	27·7	26·2	17·4	5·6
Social costs less grants	(13·5)	(10·8)	(9·8)	(11·1)	(12·9)	(13·7)	(15·9)	(16·8)	(28·8)	(61·4)
Profit on realisation of fixed assets	—	13·6	6·6	5·0	6·2	14·4	31·6	24·4	19·0	19·5
Profit/(loss) on trading	(39·4)	(98·7)	40·4	52·2	109·8	108·7	121·1	27·6	69·5	(84·5)
Interest	(43·9)	(32·2)	(36·2)	(50·0)	(78·0)	(87·0)	(138·0)	(184·7)	(256·2)	(341·0)
Taxation and other items	(0·4)	(1·3)	(1·5)	(3·2)	(3·9)	(0·6)	(2·2)	(2·2)	(0·1)	(1·2)
Extraordinary items	—	1·5	(2·7)	6·3	(0·7)	(0·2)	(0·3)	—	(20·0)	(1·6)
Deficit grant	—	—	—	—	—	—	—	159·3	149·0	428·3
Surplus/(deficit)	(83·7)	(130·7)	—	5·3	27·2	20·9	(19·4)	—	(57·8)	—

Source: NCB published accounts.

*Other activities includes non-mining activities and associated companies and partnerships.

National Coal Board—government grants

£ million

Year ended March	1972–73	1973–74	1974–75	1975–76	1976–77	1977–78	1978–79	1979–80	1980–81	1981–82
Social grants										
Social costs grants	15·4	12·7	13·8	14·4	15·2	17·0	18·2	20·9	29·7	65·4
Contribution towards increased pensions (Mineworkers' Pension Scheme)		8·3	8·3	18·0	28·2	34·0	36·1	41·1	49·3	54·3
Operating grants										
Stocking aid										
Coal		1·7	1·2		11·1	10·5	20·5			
Coke		2·0				8·3	13·7	12·9	14·2	13·4
Promotion of sales of coal to electricity generating boards		15·4				5·2	25·8	8·4	11·7	13·4
Coking coal subsidy		15·0	7·1				7·7	8·5		
Regional grants		75·0	37·8				50·0			
Deficit grant								159·3	149·0	428·3
Total	15·4	130·1	68·2	32·4	54·5	75·0	172·0	251·1	253·9	574·8

Source: The NCB.

Notes: (1) In addition to the above there were the following grants:
  (a) 1972–73—Coal Industry Act 1973 extinguished cumulative revenue deficit of £174·6 million.
  (b) 1973–74—a special government grant of £130·7 million was made to cover the deficit in this year, the results for which were affected by the overtime ban and national strike.

(2) The operating results do not reflect the expenditure borne directly by the Government through the Redundant Mineworkers' Payment Schemes provided for in the Coal Industry Act 1967, as amended, as follows:

	1972–73	1973–74	1974–75	1975–76	1976–77	1977–78	1978–79	1979–80	1980–81	1981–82
	6·4	11·1	12·4	13·5	15·7	17·6	17·8	15·7	15·6	48·6

23

APPENDIX 3.2(*b*)
(referred to in paragraph 3.8)

Description of government grants

Social grants

Social costs grants

The Secretary of State may with the consent of the Treasury make grants to the NCB with the objectives of accelerating the redeployment of employees of the NCB and the elimination of
Contribution towards increased pensions (Mineworkers' Pension Scheme)
uneconomic capacity and of meeting the extra cost of pension benefits to mineworkers made redundant and those who retired before 6 April 1975.

Operating grants

Stocking aid
  Coal
  Coke

Payment in respect of excess stocks, ie exceeding 1/12th of the annual production of the undertaking concerned.

Promotion of sales of coal to electricity generating boards

Payments to promote the sale of coal to the South of Scotland Electricity Board and the Central Electricity Generating Board.

Coking coal subsidy

Payment of grant for Coking Coal Production Aid—taking account of average cost of production and the higher of either the average indicative price (ie related to third country prices) or the NCB list price.

Regional grants

To enable the NCB to pay due regard to the needs of assisted areas under the Industry Act 1972 when planning or carrying out colliery activities (power to make grant repealed by Coal Industry Act 1980).

Deficit grant

Grant to reduce or eliminate any group deficit of the NCB. (Introduced by Coal Industry Act 1980.)

Source: The NCB.

24

APPENDIX 3.3

(referred to in paragraph 3.20)

NCB deep mines—unit operating costs 1972–73 to 1981–82

Year ended March	1972–73	1973–74	1974–75	1975–76	1976–77	1977–78	1978–79	1979–80	1980–81	1981–82
Saleable output (million tonnes)	131·8	98·7	116·8	114·5	108·4	106·2	107·7	108·6	109·6	108·2
Overall OMS (tonnes)	2·33	2·15	2·29	2·28	2·21	2·19	2·24	2·31	2·32	2·40
Net proceeds (excluding social and operating grants) £/te	6·87	7·06	11·11	15·55	18·72	21·34	23·06	27·38	32·83	35·59
Operating costs	£/te	£/te	£/te	£/te	£/te	£/te	£/te	£/te	£/te	£/te
Wages	2·74	3·31	4·33	5·54	6·15	6·85	8·36	9·54	11·39	12·20
Wages charges	0·98	1·62	1·89	2·92	3·47	3·99	4·25	4·90	5·69	6·62
Materials and repairs	1·61	2·12	2·68	3·60	4·33	5·25	5·62	6·32	7·37	7·84
Power, heat & light	0·31	0·39	0·52	0·70	0·84	0·99	1·09	1·23	1·51	1·73
Salaries & related expenses	0·28	0·37	0·41	0·51	0·62	0·70	0·75	0·88	1·11	1·28
Other colliery expenses	0·53	0·79	0·91	1·06	1·34	1·61	1·84	2·87	3·35	4·56
Overheads and services	0·65	0·83	1·00	1·26	1·54	1·82	1·99	2·28	2·72	3·08
Depreciation	0·45	0·41	0·34	0·61	0·74	0·87	0·97	1·36	1·74	2·17
Total costs	7·55	9·84	12·08	16·20	19·03	22·08	24·87	29·38	34·88	39·48
Gross social costs (included above)	0·22	0·23	0·20	0·22	0·25	0·28	0·31	0·33	0·50	1·14
Total costs, excluding gross social costs	7·33	9·61	11·88	15·98	18·78	21·80	24·56	29·05	34·38	38·34

Source: The NCB.

Notes: (1) Net proceeds represents production valued at list prices net of market rebates, including sundry sales and service charges, after adjustment for stocks designed to achieve a stock valuation based on the principle of the lower of cost or market value in accordance with normal accounting practice.

(2) From 1980–81 operating costs reflect the change in accounting policy of capitalisation of costs of mine drivages with a life in excess of five years.

(referred to in paragraph 3.25)

NCB deep mines

Area operating results—saleable output 1976–77 to 1981–82

						million tonnes
Area	*1976–77*	*1977–78*	*1978–79*	*1979–80*	*1980–81*	*1981–82*
North-East	13·1	12·8	13·2	14·0	14·1	13·4
North Nottinghamshire	10·7	11·1	11·3	11·9	12·0	12·3
Western	11·3	10·8	11·2	11·1	11·2	11·1
South Midlands	8·8	8·5	8·7	8·5	8·5	8·6
South Nottinghamshire	9·1	8·9	8·8	8·7	8·8	8·5
North Derbyshire	7·3	7·4	7·5	7·6	8·2	8·5
Barnsley	7·3	7·5	7·5	8·0	8·3	8·4
North Yorkshire	8·2	8·2	8·4	8·1	8·5	8·3
South Wales	7·8	7·5	7·9	7·6	7·7	7·6
Scottish	9·1	8·4	8·3	8·0	7·7	7·2
South Yorkshire	7·8	7·6	7·8	7·6	7·4	7·2
Doncaster	7·9	7·5	7·1	7·5	7·2	7·1

Source: The NCB.

Note: Figures from 1979–80 onwards are affected by revised treatment of capitalisation of drivages.

NCB deep mines

Area operating results—OMS—1976–77 to 1981–82

						tonnes
Area	*1976–77*	*1977–78*	*1978–79*	*1979–80*	*1980–81*	*1981–82*
North Derbyshire	2·83	2·84	2·90	2·99	3·21	3·33
North Nottinghamshire	2·89	2·96	2·92	3·08	3·04	3·17
North Yorkshire	2·57	2·56	2·57	2·50	2·68	2·80
Barnsley	2·26	2·31	2·43	2·56	2·62	2·71
South Nottinghamshire	2·75	2·67	2·61	2·64	2·68	2·68
South Midlands	2·60	2·47	2·50	2·45	2·36	2·52
Western	2·18	2·14	2·24	2·35	2·35	2·45
Doncaster	2·45	2·30	2·28	2·29	2·18	2·27
South Yorkshire	2·19	2·17	2·25	2·24	2·17	2·22
North-East	1·85	1·83	1·87	2·07	2·07	2·07
Scottish	1·96	1·91	1·96	1·98	1·92	2·00
South Wales	1·32	1·29	1·41	1·39	1·46	1·47

	1976–77 =100		*1981–82*
North Derbyshire	100		118
North Nottinghamshire	100		110
North Yorkshire	100		109
Barnsley	100		120
South Nottinghamshire	100		97
South Midlands	100		97
Western	100		112
Doncaster	100		93
South Yorkshire	100		101
North-East	100		112
Scottish	100		102
South Wales	100		111

Source: The NCB.

NCB deep mines

Area operating results—operating costs 1976–77 to 1981–82

£ per tonne

Area	1976–77	1977–78	1978–79	1979–80	1980–81	1981–82
South Wales	30·1	35·0	36·1	45·0	51·4	58·8
North-East	21·0	24·3	27·5	30·6	36·9	42·8
Scottish	19·6	23·3	25·7	30·2	37·2	42·6
Western	21·1	24·9	26·9	30·5	36·5	40·5
South Yorkshire	18·6	21·6	24·5	29·5	36·0	40·3
Doncaster	17·6	20·8	24·9	29·4	36·4	39·4
Barnsley	18·9	21·2	24·4	28·5	33·5	37·4
North Yorkshire	17·0	19·6	22·6	29·3	33·3	37·2
South Midlands	16·9	19·9	21·8	27·2	33·3	36·2
South Nottinghamshire	15·7	18·7	21·9	26·4	31·0	36·0
North Derbyshire	16·1	18·8	21·4	25·1	28·3	33·8
North Nottinghamshire	15·4	17·4	20·6	23·2	27·9	32·1

Area	1976–77 =100	1981–82
South Wales	100	195
North-East	100	204
Scottish	100	217
Western	100	192
South Yorkshire	100	217
Doncaster	100	224
Barnsley	100	198
North Yorkshire	100	219
South Midlands	100	214
South Nottinghamshire	100	229
North Derbyshire	100	210
North Nottinghamshire	100	208

Source: The NCB.

NCB deep mines

Area operating results—operating surplus/(loss)
1976–77 to 1981–82

£ *per tonne*

Area	1976–77	1977–78	1978–79	1979–80	1980–81*	1981–82
North Nottinghamshire	2·7	4·1	2·7	4·5	5·1	3·1
North Derbyshire	0·7	0·8	(0·3)	0·1	3·2	0·1
South Yorkshire	2·6	2·6	1·3	0·7	(1·3)	(0·8)
Western	(0·9)	(1·7)	(2·2)	(1·3)	(1·8)	(1·4)
Barnsley	0·1	(0·1)	(2·3)	(2·7)	(1·3)	(1·8)
South Nottinghamshire	0·4	(0·0)	(1·4)	(1·5)	0·1	(2·6)
South Midlands	1·0	0·7	0·7	(0·8)	(1·3)	(2·7)
North Yorkshire	(0·3)	(0·6)	(1·7)	(4·3)	(2·0)	(2·7)
Doncaster	0·4	(0·6)	(2·5)	(2·2)	(3·0)	(2·9)
North-East	(0·2)	(1·1)	(1·5)	(0·7)	(2·4)	(3·8)
Scottish	(1·6)	(1·9)	(1·5)	(2·5)	(3·7)	(5·5)
South Wales	(2·7)	(4·3)	(2·4)	(7·8)	(9·4)	(13·2)

Source: The NCB.

*Market rebates, covering rebates to customers including exports, have always been charged to Areas but there was a change in the system from 1980–81. These are now allocated from a national pool.

(referred to in paragraph 3.31)

NCB deep mines

Colliery operating results 1981–82—(1) Scottish Area (12* collieries)

Colliery	Saleable output ('000 tonnes)	Overall OMS (tonnes)	Net proceeds (£/te)	Operating costs (£/te)	Operating surplus/(loss) (£/te)
1. Cardowan	267	1·30	31·6	69·9	(38·3)
2. Sorn	57	1·33	36·6	58·1	(21·5)
3. Polkemmet	390	1·39	45·5	54·5	(9·0)
4. Frances	254	1·85	35·3	53·1	(17·8)
5. Barony	227	2·00	36·4	50·2	(13·8)
6. Killoch	698	1·58	32·3	49·0	(16·7)
7. Comrie	374	1·61	31·7	48·3	(16·6)
8. Highhouse	118	1·81	39·9	47·3	(7·4)
9. Seafield	848	1·98	35·4	44·1	(8·7)
10. Bilston Glen	892	2·06	38·1	42·7	(4·6)
11. Monktonhall	895	2·31	30·1	38·3	(8·2)
12. Longannet Complex	1,955	3·19	29·7	31·2	(1·5)

Source: The NCB.

*Excludes two collieries that ceased production during year.

NCB deep mines

Colliery operating results 1981–82—(2) North-East Area (22 collieries)

Colliery	Saleable output ('000 tonnes)	Overall OMS (tonnes)	Net proceeds (£/te)	Operating costs (£/te)	Operating surplus/(loss) (£/te)
1. Horden	597	1·47	44·1	68·5	(24·4)
2. Herrington	254	1·21	44·5	65·8	(21·2)
3. Sacriston	76	1·23	38·4	64·9	(26·4)
4. Marley Hill*	213	1·34	43·5	58·8	(15·2)
5. East Hetton	289	1·49	42·9	58·1	(15·2)
6. Bearpark	140	1·52	31·3	51·0	(19·7)
7. Lynemouth	546	1·76	32·3	49·4	(17·1)
8. Hawthorn Complex	1,219	1·82	36·9	49·3	(12·4)
9. Brenkley	231	1·71	33·4	47·2	(13·9)
10. Ashington	376	2·25	34·3	46·3	(12·0)
11. Shilbottle	168	1·67	36·7	45·6	(8·8)
12. South Hetton	161	2·06	32·9	45·2	(12·3)
13. Wearmouth	1,105	2·25	43·5	44·1	(0·7)
14. Easington	1,291	2·22	37·1	43·2	(6·0)
15. Vane Tempest	525	2·48	35·6	41·3	(5·8)
16. Bates	890	2·35	32·5	41·2	(8·6)
17. Seaham	264	2·44	36·2	39·9	(3·7)
18. Dawdon	1,061	2·31	37·8	38·8	(1·0)
19. Westoe	1,412	2·67	35·4	37·7	(2·3)
20. Boldon	377	2·36	38·4	36·4	2·0
21. Whittle	337	2·79	36·7	32·4	4·3
22. Ellington	1,763	3·75	32·8	27·2	5·6

Source: The NCB.

*Run down and eventual closure announced by the NCB 14 July 1982 (due to exhaustion of reserves).

APPENDIX 3.5(*c*)
(referred to in paragraph 3.31)

NCB deep mines

Colliery operating results 1981–82—(3) North Yorkshire Area (14 collieries)

Colliery	Saleable output ('000 tonnes)	Overall OMS (tonnes)	Net proceeds (£/te)	Operating costs (£/te)	Operating surplus/(loss) (£/te)
1. Rothwell	259	1·84	36·2	54·2	(18·0)
2. Ackton Hall	619	2·11	35·9	47·7	(11·8)
3. Glasshoughton	261	2·02	31·7	46·3	(14·6)
4. Fryston	503	2·19	33·7	43·1	(9·4)
5. Newmarket Silks	310	2·37	32·8	42·1	(9·3)
6. Prince of Wales	945	3·40	31·5	38·8	(7·3)
7. Park Hill	260	2·52	33·5	38·6	(5·1)
8. Wheldale	510	2·71	34·5	38·2	(3·7)
9. Allerton Bywater	741	2·46	32·1	36·4	(4·3)
10. Savile	321	2·69	35·1	36·3	(1·2)
11. Sharlston	787	2·99	32·7	32·9	(0·2)
12. Nostell	398	3·19	31·3	30·9	0·4
13. Kellingley	1,815	3·85	33·8	30·7	3·1
14. Ledston Luck	385	3·37	33·0	26·3	6·7

Source: The NCB.

APPENDIX 3.5(*d*)
(referred to in paragraph 3.31)

NCB deep mines

Colliery operating results 1981–82—(4) Doncaster Area (10 collieries)

Colliery	Saleable output ('000 tonnes)	Overall OMS (tonnes)	Net proceeds (£/te)	Operating costs (£/te)	Operating surplus/(loss) (£/te)
1. Hickleton	363	1·57	41·2	53·5	(12·3)
2. Hatfield	567	1·74	36·2	53·0	(16·8)
3. Brodsworth	883	1·79	37·6	47·5	(9·9)
4. Bentley	479	2·18	32·8	42·9	(10·1)
5. Frickley/South Elmsall	834	2·19	34·8	39·0	(4·2)
6. Yorkshire Main	713	2·23	39·5	38·9	0·6
7. Goldthorpe/Highgate	661	2·40	29·9	38·9	(9·0)
8. Markham Main	724	2·40	37·4	37·5	(0·1)
9. Askern	819	3·20	34·7	30·6	4·1
10. Rossington	1,074	3·26	35·9	27·7	8·2

Source: The NCB.

33

APPENDIX 3.5(*e*)
(referred to in paragraph 3.31)

NCB deep mines

Colliery operating results 1981–82—(5) Barnsley Area (16 collieries)

Colliery	Saleable output ('000 tonnes)	Overall OMS (tonnes)	Net proceeds (£/te)	Operating costs (£/te)	Operating surplus/(loss) (£/te)
1. Barrow	452	1·56	42·4	62·0	(19·6)
2. Emley Moor	110	1·77	45·6	49·6	(4·0)
3. Bullcliffe Wood	191	2·80	29·0	48·4	(19·4)
4. Woolley	748	2·00	37·3	46·1	(8·8)
5. Darfield Main	326	2·04	35·2	42·9	(7·7)
6. Dodworth	583	2·21	33·9	42·8	(8·9)
7. North Gawber	388	2·45	35·5	37·8	(2·3)
8. Park Mill	248	3·48	34·7	35·2	(0·5)
9. South Kirkby	1,006	3·21	34·8	33·8	1·0
10. Grimethorpe	1,076	2·82	37·1	33·4	3·7
11. Ferrymoor/Riddings	480	3·78	33·4	32·9	0·5
12. Caphouse/ Denby Grange	383	3·56	38·1	32·6	5·5
13. Houghton Main	1,137	3·10	36·8	32·3	4·5
14. Dearne Valley	273	3·32	34·8	31·5	3·3
15. Kinsley Drift	395	5·12	32·4	29·3	3·1
16. Royston Drift	557	4·99	27·6	26·8	0·8

Source: The NCB.

NCB deep mines

Colliery operating results 1981–82—(6) South Yorkshire Area (17 collieries)

Colliery	Saleable output ('000 tonnes)	Overall OMS (tonnes)	Net proceeds (£/te)	Operating costs (£/te)	Operating surplus/(loss) (£/te)
1. Kilnhurst	138	1·29	41·0	66·6	(25·6)
2. Manvers	389	1·57	40·9	56·6	(15·7)
3. Cadeby	328	1·63	36·6	53·6	(17·0)
4. Elsecar	259	1·69	36·2	51·6	(15·4)
5. Cortonwood	281	1·63	44·3	50·5	(6·2)
6. Barnburgh	468	2·24	36·9	45·6	(8·7)
7. Dinnington	367	1·88	43·7	45·0	(1·3)
8. Brookhouse	263	1·97	43·3	43·8	(0·5)
9. Treeton	311	2·02	35·1	43·4	(8·3)
10. Thurcroft	375	2·39	43·7	39·2	4·5
11. Wath	401	2·46	40·5	38·6	1·9
12. Steetley	243	2·24	35·2	38·1	(2·9)
13. Kiveton Park	366	2·34	32·4	37·5	(5·1)
14. Silverwood	853	2·67	44·3	34·8	9·5
15. Maltby	822	2·79	35·4	31·8	3·6
16. Shireoaks	434	3·38	32·1	29·5	2·6
17. Manton	879	3·52	36·4	28·7	7·7

Source: The NCB.

APPENDIX 3.5(g)
(referred to in paragraph 3.31)

NCB deep mines

Colliery operating results 1981–82—(7) North Derbyshire Area (11 collieries)

Colliery	Saleable output ('000 tonnes)	Overall OMS (tonnes)	Net proceeds (£/te)	Operating costs (£/te)	Operating surplus/(loss) (£/te)
1. Warsop	697	2·40	36·1	44·8	(8·7)
2. Arkwright	639	3·05	37·1	35·9	1·2
3. Whitwell	516	2·78	33·4	35·7	(2·3)
4. Bolsover	693	3·16	39·4	33·7	5·7
5. Pleasley	462	3·50	28·1	32·6	(4·5)
6. Markham	1,528	3·02	34·7	31·5	3·2
7. Renishaw Park	439	3·49	32·9	30·3	2·6
8. Westthorpe	503	3·44	28·0	28·4	(0·4)
9. Shirebrook	1,681	4·19	33·1	26·3	6·8
10. Ireland	657	3·92	34·3	27·5	6·8
11. High Moor	595	4·83	30·3	25·4	4·9

Source: The NCB.

APPENDIX 3.5(*h*)
(*referred to in paragraph 3.31*)

NCB deep mines

Colliery operating results 1981–82—(8) North Nottinghamshire Area (14 collieries)

Colliery	Saleable output ('000 tonnes)	Overall OMS (tonnes)	Net proceeds (£/te)	Operating costs (£/te)	Operating surplus/(loss) (£/te)
1. Blidworth	527	2·17	39·6	44·7	(5·1)
2. Rufford	693	2·13	42·0	42·9	(0·9)
3. Mansfield	831	2·46	40·5	40·9	(0·4)
4. Sutton	438	2·46	35·1	40·0	(4·9)
5. Clipstone	873	2·73	41·9	35·3	6·6
6. Bevercotes	883	2·85	34·8	35·3	(0·5)
7. Harworth	773	3·09	35·3	31·4	3·9
8. Silverhill	789	2·91	33·6	31·4	2·2
9. Cresswell	762	3·14	34·2	28·9	5·3
10. Bilsthorpe	970	3·33	32·4	28·8	3·6
11. Sherwood	881	3·88	34·0	28·1	5·9
12. Ollerton	1,048	4·16	34·9	24·6	10·3
13. Welbeck	1,156	4·13	33·5	24·0	9·5
14. Thoresby	1,640	5·12	33·7	21·9	11·8

Source: The NCB.

(referred to in paragraph 3.31)

NCB deep mines

Colliery operating results 1981–82—(9) South Nottinghamshire Area (11 collieries)

Colliery	Saleable output ('000 tonnes)	Overall OMS (tonnes)	Net proceeds (£/te)	Operating costs (£/te)	Operating surplus/(loss) (£/te)
1. Babbington	501	2·02	30·6	51·2	(20·6)
2. Newstead	615	2·15	32·7	41·6	(8·9)
3. Linby	623	2·73	37·8	38·2	(0·4)
4. Bentinck	1,129	2·80	33·5	37·0	(3·5)
5. Annesley	439	2·45	33·6	36·7	(3·1)
6. Gedling	769	2·35	37·9	35·9	2·0
7. Calverton	787	2·52	35·4	33·9	1·5
8. Hucknall	760	3·08	29·7	33·7	(4·0)
9. Moorgreen	634	2·70	33·4	33·5	(0·1)
10. Pye Hill	821	3·53	32·6	27·9	4·7
11. Cotgrave	1,205	3·21	31·0	27·6	3·4

Source: The NCB.

NCB deep mines

Colliery operating results 1981–82—(10) South Midlands Area (17 collieries)

Colliery	Saleable output ('000 tonnes)	Overall OMS (tonnes)	Net proceeds (£/te)	Operating costs (£/te)	Operating surplus/(loss) (£/te)
1. Snowdon	129	0·69	43·6	112·2	(68·6)
2. Tilmanstone	240	1·26	43·1	70·1	(27·0)
3. Betteshanger	423	1·66	42·2	53·2	(11·0)
4. Snibston	251	1·69	29·8	49·5	(19·7)
5. Measham	223	2·12	29·6	42·9	(13·3)
6. South Leicester	270	2·15	28·9	38·9	(10·0)
7. Desford	406	2·28	26·4	38·7	(12·3)
8. Cadley Hill	415	2·24	34·2	37·1	(2·9)
9. Donisthorpe	539	2·48	32·4	36·0	(3·6)
10. Rawdon	615	2·41	32·4	35·7	(3·3)
11. Baddesley	566	2·53	30·0	34·9	(4·9)
12. Birch Coppice	560	2·47	29·9	34·5	(4·6)
13. Coventry	887	3·01	35·6	30·8	4·8
14. Whitwick	540	2·97	29·6	30·7	(1·1)
15. Ellistown	429	3·46	30·2	28·6	1·6
16. Daw Mill	1,119	4·21	38·2	25·7	12·5
17. Bagworth	950	5·56	30·3	21·6	8·7

Source: The NCB.

APPENDIX 3.5(*k*)
(referred to in paragraph 3.31)

NCB deep mines

Colliery operating results 1981–82—(11) Western Area (21 collieries)

Colliery	Saleable output ('000 tonnes)	Overall OMS (tonnes)	Net proceeds (£/te)	Operating costs (£/te)	Operating surplus/(loss) (£/te)
1. Bold	451	1·61	38·0	62·5	(24·5)
2. Victoria	158	1·49	34·5	58·7	(24·2)
3. Holditch	278	1·89	45·5	57·1	(11·6)
4. Wolstanton	457	1·68	42·2	55·5	(13·3)
5. Bersham	212	1·89	39·4	54·7	(15·3)
6. Cronton	227	1·84	37·5	50·0	(12·5)
7. Bickershaw	366	1·92	36·7	47·9	(11·2)
8. Sutton Manor	379	2·14	39·2	47·7	(8·5)
9. West Cannock	311	1·93	33·5	46·7	(13·2)
10. Agecroft	441	2·17	37·4	43·2	(5·8)
11. Lea Hall	1,076	2·38	34·0	41·4	(7·4)
12. Littleton	958	2·40	36·1	39·9	(3·8)
13. Haig	471	2·41	43·7	39·6	4·1
14. Parkside	854	2·47	42·8	39·0	3·8
15. Golborne	515	2·92	37·3	35·9	1·4
16. Silverdale	523	3·23	34·2	34·2	(0·0)
17. Parsonage	355	2·90	37·1	33·4	3·7
18. Hem Heath	1,240	3·39	36·3	32·6	3·7
19. Point of Ayr	472	3·14	36·1	30·2	5·9
20. Florence	1,016	3·68	36·6	29·6	7·0
21. Hapton Valley	173	3·56	40·2	28·2	12·0

Source: The NCB.

NCB deep mines

Colliery operating results 1981–82—(12) South Wales Area (33 collieries)

Colliery	Saleable output ('000 tonnes)	Overall OMS (tonnes)	Net proceeds (£/te)	Operating costs (£/te)	Operating surplus/(loss) (£/te)
1. Treforgan	62	0·64	48·2	153·0	(104·8)
2. Tymaur/Lewis Merthyr	76	0·59	44·7	128·6	(83·9)
3. Abertillery	110	0·68	43·3	114·3	(71·0)
4. Wyndham/Western	124	0·89	42·8	88·2	(45·4)
5. Nantgarw	165	1·30	44·8	87·3	(42·5)
6. Tower	134	0·91	53·8	87·0	(33·2)
7. Cynheidre	245	1·11	57·4	81·5	(24·1)
8. Bedwas	149	1·09	41·9	81·3	(39·4)
9. Penrikyber	140	0·98	45·8	79·6	(33·8)
10. Aberpergwm	74	1·23	53·1	77·5	(24·4)
11. Mardy	189	1·07	52·0	76·6	(24·6)
12. Abernant	189	1·14	53·7	74·5	(20·8)
13. Oakdale	237	1·23	43·6	74·3	(30·7)
14. Garw	198	1·22	41·7	72·7	(31·0)
15. Blaenserchan	116	1·28	42·8	70·8	(28·0)
16. Markham	164	1·34	43·7	69·9	(26·2)
17. Blaengwrach	63	1·27	53·3	67·6	(14·3)
18. Celynen South	132	1·32	43·8	66·3	(22·5)
19. L Wind/Abercynon	355	1·44	45·4	61·2	(15·8)
20. Brynlliw	229	1·55	39·8	59·6	(19·8)
21. Celynen North	208	1·64	43·2	58·5	(15·3)
22. Britannia	142	1·43	38·6	57·9	(19·3)
23. St Johns	263	1·49	34·4	55·0	(20·6)
24. Six Bells	173	1·77	42·7	52·9	(10·2)
25. Cwm/Coedely	504	1·85	47·3	52·3	(5·0)
26. Merthyr Vale	261	1·77	41·3	51·5	(10·2)
27. Marine	280	2·10	42·7	46·2	(3·5)
28. Penallta	255	1·93	41·6	42·9	(1·3)
29. Betws New Mine	589	4·40	52·7	42·2	10·5
30. Trelewis	266	3·45	25·5	38·4	(12·9)
31. Taff Merthyr	448	2·91	33·3	35·5	(2·2)
32. Deep Navigation	422	2·81	38·3	32·9	5·4
33. Blaenant	450	3·16	27·2	32·1	(4·9)

Source: The NCB.

41

NCB deep mines

Colliery operating surplus/(loss) 1976–77 to 1981–82—(1) Scottish Area (12* collieries)

£ per tonne

Colliery	1976–77	1977–78	1978–79	1979–80	1980–81	1981–82
1. Cardowan	(9·7)	(13·1)	(21·6)	(21·8)	(27·0)	(38·3)
2. Sorn	(3·2)	(6·6)	(6·6)	(2·5)	(22·9)	(21·5)
3. Barony	(9·1)	(4·5)	(7·1)	(13·3)	(5·5)	(13·8)
4. Killoch	(4·3)	(5·1)	(6·6)	(10·8)	(10·2)	(16·7)
5. Seafield	(6·1)	(6·0)	(8·6)	(7·4)	(13·0)	(8·7)
6. Bilston Glen	(0·8)	(1·0)	(1·6)	(2·0)	(1·8)	(4·6)
7. Frances	(2·4)	(6·3)	(14·9)	0·0	(4·6)	(17·8)
8. Highhouse	(1·4)	(1·7)	(4·7)	0·3	(3·0)	(7·4)
9. Longannet Complex	(1·1)	0·5	(0·2)	(0·4)	(1·3)	(1·5)
10. Polkemmet	3·2	(8·2)	2·4	(5·0)	(6·5)	(9·0)
11. Comrie	2·1	1·1	(4·0)	3·5	(1·5)	(16·6)
12. Monktonhall	0·5	(0·3)	0·4	2·2	(7·6)	(8·2)

Source: The NCB.

*Excludes two collieries that ceased production during 1981–82.

APPENDIX 3.6(*b*)
(referred to in paragraph 3.31)

NCB deep mines

Colliery operating surplus/(loss) 1976–77 to 1981–82—(2) North-East Area (22 collieries)

£ per tonne

Colliery	1976–77	1977–78	1978–79	1979–80	1980–81	1981–82
1. Horden	(6·2)	(2·1)	(7·8)	(15·5)	(13·1)	(24·4)
2. Lynemouth	(1·4)	(2·3)	(5·0)	(6·8)	(11·1)	(17·1)
3. Brenkley	(1·5)	(1·7)	(1·2)	(3·8)	(8·8)	(13·9)
4. Ashington	(4·4)	(7·6)	(4·4)	(9·4)	(8·2)	(12·0)
5. Shilbottle	(3·3)	(2·4)	(6·8)	(8·0)	(9·7)	(8·8)
6. South Hetton	(4·2)	(10·2)	(12·9)	(35·5)	(5·7)	(12·3)
7. Easington	(3·1)	(17·3)	(11·0)	(2·5)	(0·2)	(6·0)
8. Bates	(4·0)	(4·7)	(7·6)	(6·4)	(13·6)	(8·6)
9. Hawthorn Complex	(1·1)	(0·3)	(3·9)	(4·1)	(8·0)	(12·4)
10. Bearpark	1·5	(1·8)	(2·5)	(7·9)	(17·5)	(19·7)
11. Vane Tempest	(0·1)	(1·4)	(1·6)	0·8	(6·8)	(5·8)
12. Boldon	(3·4)	(3·6)	(4·9)	(4·3)	(2·2)	2·0
13. Whittle	(1·1)	(2·9)	(5·0)	(5·3)	(5·0)	4·3
14. Sacriston	0·6	2·1	(5·6)	(7·2)	(22·6)	(26·4)
15. East Hetton	1·5	1·6	(5·4)	(12·6)	(14·0)	(15·2)
16. Westoe	(3·6)	(0·3)	(2·7)	0·2	0·9	(2·3)
17. Herrington	(2·2)	4·6	5·0	4·9	(9·1)	(21·2)
18. Seaham	4·4	0·5	(1·5)	2·6	(0·3)	(3·7)
19. Marley Hill	3·0	4·4	0·8	2·0	(16·1)	(15·2)
20. Wearmouth	7·2	9·0	7·1	4·1	0·7	(0·7)
21. Dawdon	3·7	5·3	7·0	9·1	8·0	(1·0)
22. Ellington	3·8	4·0	2·6	6·3	7·0	5·6

Source: The NCB.

43

(referred to in paragraph 3.31)

NCB deep mines

Colliery operating surplus/(loss) 1976–77 to 1981–82—(3) North Yorkshire Area (14 collieries)

£ per tonne

Colliery	1976–77	1977–78	1978–79	1979–80	1980–81	1981–82
1. Rothwell	(0·4)	(2·2)	(3·9)	(2·9)	(6·4)	(18·0)
2. Ackton Hall	(0·3)	(0·4)	(3·8)	(6·0)	(14·6)	(11·8)
3. Fryston	(2·2)	(0·9)	(2·2)	(0·9)	(5·2)	(9·4)
4. Newmarket Silks	(0·3)	(1·9)	(6·8)	(2·5)	(2·3)	(9·3)
5. Prince of Wales	(2·7)	(20·4)	(0·7)	(4·3)	(10·1)	(7·3)
6. Wheldale	(1·2)	(4·3)	(4·2)	(13·3)	(4·7)	(3·7)
7. Glasshoughton	(1·2)	(0·0)	0·5	(1·0)	(0·9)	(14·6)
8. Park Hill	(5·5)	4·7	2·2	(6·8)	(16·8)	(5·1)
9. Allerton Bywater	4·1	1·9	(2·3)	4·3	(8·3)	(4·3)
10. Savile	3·0	2·0	1·0	(4·2)	(1·8)	(1·2)
11. Sharlston	2·3	0·5	0·8	(4·6)	(1·4)	(0·2)
12. Kellingley	1·7	5·2	3·6	(2·3)	5·3	3·1
13. Ledston Luck	4·6	6·3	(2·9)	2·5	9·6	6·7
14. Nostell	1·0	5·1	1·0	2·5	0·3	0·4

Source: The NCB.

(referred to in paragraph 3.31)

NCB deep mines

Colliery operating surplus/(loss) 1976–77 to 1981–82—(4)
Doncaster Area (10 collieries)

						£ per tonne
Colliery	*1976–77*	*1977–78*	*1978–79*	*1979–80*	*1980–81*	*1981–82*
1. Hatfield	(0·5)	(0·4)	(4·5)	(1·0)	(10·4)	(16·8)
2. Hickleton	(5·1)	(14·4)	(8·4)	3·4	(2·8)	(12·3)
3. Bentley	1·6	(2·6)	(1·2)	0·2	(6·1)	(10·1)
4. Yorkshire Main	(2·7)	(0·6)	(7·7)	1·4	(1·3)	0·6
5. Markham Main	2·5	(5·9)	(21·8)	(2·3)	6·1	(0·1)
6. Askern	0·7	(2·2)	(6·9)	(5·5)	(6·7)	4·1
7. Frickley/South Elmsall	(1·1)	(0·1)	0·6	1·0	(3·7)	(4·2)
8. Brodsworth	0·5	3·0	1·8	(3·0)	(1·7)	(9·9)
9. Goldthorpe/Highgate	3·9	3·1	1·4	(5·0)	(8·8)	(9·0)
10. Rossington	0·7	3·4	1·9	(1·7)	(6·6)	8·2

Source: The NCB.

NCB deep mines

Colliery operating surplus/(loss) 1976–77 to 1981–82—(5)
Barnsley Area (16 collieries)

						£ per tonne
Colliery	1976–77	1977–78	1978–79	1979–80	1980–81	1981–82
1. Barrow	(7·2)	(22·5)	(16·8)	(13·4)	(18·8)	(19·6)
2. Dodworth	(0·9)	(2·1)	(2·3)	(1·7)	(2·5)	(8·9)
3. Darfield Main	(1·0)	0·5	(0·2)	(1·7)	(0·9)	(7·7)
4. South Kirkby	(4·4)	(1·0)	(5·9)	(7·4)	(0·5)	1·0
5. Park Mill	0·7	0·6	(3·0)	(3·8)	(14·5)	(0·5)
6. Woolley	3·5	3·5	(7·0)	(4·1)	(13·1)	(8·8)
7. North Gawber	2·2	4·2	(0·3)	(10·2)	(11·9)	(2·3)
8. Bullcliffe Wood	2·2	2·2	(1·9)	3·1	(15·7)	(19·4)
9. Ferrymoor/Riddings	5·1	(3·0)	(5·4)	(8·2)	2·0	0·5
10. Emley Moor	2·9	4·0	4·7	4·6	(4·7)	(4·0)
11. Dearne Valley	(1·7)	0·4	3·4	3·9	(0·1)	3·3
12. Kinsley Drift				(88·1)	(40·3)	3·1
13. Royston Drift	(0·8)	1·2	2·9	(0·4)	4·5	0·8
14. Houghton Main	1·5	2·1	(3·8)	0·7	3·3	4·5
15. Grimethorpe	1·0	4·7	1·6	3·6	8·1	3·7
16. Caphouse/Denby Grange	2·8	6·9	6·9	6·9	2·6	5·5

Source: The NCB.

46

NCB deep mines

Colliery operating surplus/(loss) 1976–77 to 1981–82—(6) South Yorkshire Area (17 collieries)

						£ per tonne
Colliery	*1976–77*	*1977–78*	*1978–79*	*1979–80*	*1980–81*	*1981–82*
1. Kilnhurst	(16·3)	(7·3)	(17·7)	(7·6)	(12·9)	(25·6)
2. Manvers	(1·7)	(5·6)	(16·3)	(4·8)	(4·5)	(15·7)
3. Cadeby	(7·9)	(0·7)	(8·8)	(16·1)	(22·7)	(17·0)
4. Brookhouse	(7·2)	(53·2)	(55·6)	(64·8)	(27·6)	(0·5)
5. Treeton	0·3	4·0	(1·8)	(2·2)	(0·9)	(8·3)
6. Dinnington	(2·0)	(0·1)	7·2	5·5	(5·4)	(1·3)
7. Kiveton Park	(2·5)	(2·2)	3·8	5·0	5·5	(5·1)
8. Elsecar	5·7	4·3	3·2	3·4	(12·0)	(15·4)
9. Cortonwood	2·3	2·5	2·6	3·5	(12·8)	(6·2)
10. Barnburgh	0·9	(0·2)	3·2	2·9	1·2	(8·7)
11. Thurcroft	5·7	3·8	(1·7)	2·9	(0·8)	4·5
12. Shireoaks	2·8	2·4	(1·6)	(2·5)	5·0	2·6
13. Steetley	2·7	4·3	4·3	4·5	2·5	(2·9)
14. Maltby	6·4	8·7	(1·7)	4·9	1·0	3·6
15. Wath	3·4	3·4	1·3	1·0	2·3	1·9
16. Silverwood	9·3	4·9	6·7	5·1	0·3	9·5
17. Manton	7·6	10·9	9·3	8·1	5·3	7·7

Source: The NCB.

Appendix 3.6(g)
(referred to in paragraph 3.31)

NCB deep mines

Colliery operating surplus/(loss) 1976–77 to 1981–82—(7) North Derbyshire Area (11 collieries)

						£ per tonne
Colliery	1976–77	1977–78	1978–79	1979–80	1980–81	1981–82
1. Pleasley	(1·8)	(0·7)	(4·0)	(3·4)	(1·4)	(4·5)
2. Westthorpe	(0·5)	(0·3)	(0·5)	(0·4)	(1·2)	(0·4)
3. Whitwell	(7·6)	(7·8)	(7·3)	(3·2)	0·1	(2·3)
4. Warsop	1·7	0·3	(1·9)	(2·3)	2·6	(8·7)
5. Renishaw Park	(5·4)	(3·3)	2·3	(0·4)	3·8	2·6
6. Arkwright	1·2	2·0	(2·4)	(7·0)	2·1	1·2
7. High Moor	(0·1)	3·7	(0·8)	4·2	2·5	4·9
8. Shirebrook	1·3	1·0	(0·3)	2·5	3·8	6·8
9. Bolsover	3·3	3·5	4·4	4·8	6·4	5·7
10. Markham	3·2	2·7	1·1	3·4	3·2	3·2
11. Ireland	3·8	4·2	5·0	4·5	6·1	6·8

Source: The NCB.

(referred to in paragraph 3.31)

NCB deep mines

Colliery operating surplus/(loss) 1976–77 to 1981–82—(8) North Nottinghamshire Area (14 collieries)

						£ per tonne
Colliery	1976–77	1977–78	1978–79	1979–80	1980–81	1981–82
1. Sutton	(1·0)	(6·1)	(3·8)	(15·4)	(1·0)	(4·9)
2. Blidworth	0·1	(2·6)	(1·7)	(3·5)	(4·7)	(5·1)
3. Rufford	0·4	1·5	(0·1)	(2·1)	(4·4)	(0·9)
4. Bilsthorpe	(4·5)	(0·5)	(10·9)	0·7	(4·7)	3·6
5. Bevercotes	(0·0)	3·5	2·2	2·3	0·6	(0·5)
6. Harworth	3·6	(1·3)	0·5	5·5	(6·1)	3·9
7. Mansfield	5·4	4·9	4·3	5·8	4·7	(0·4)
8. Creswell	1·0	2·9	(0·6)	3·5	5·2	5·3
9. Clipstone	8·8	9·8	6·1	10·5	7·6	6·6
10. Silverhill	2·5	7·4	8·9	2·2	5·1	2·2
11. Sherwood	6·5	6·3	2·5	7·3	4·8	5·9
12. Ollerton	1·5	3·9	5·4	10·8	13·0	10·3
13. Welbeck	7·2	9·0	6·5	9·2	9·0	9·5
14. Thoresby	5·2	7·1	7·5	10·7	13·3	11·8

Source: The NCB.

(referred to in paragraph 3.31)

NCB deep mines

Colliery operating surplus/(loss) 1976–77 to 1981–82—(9) South Nottinghamshire Area (11 collieries)

						£ per tonne
Colliery	*1976–77*	*1977–78*	*1978–79*	*1979–80*	*1980–81*	*1981–82*
1. Babbington	(3·0)	(4·2)	(4·5)	(8·1)	(11·9)	(20·6)
2. Moorgreen	(1·1)	(6·3)	(6·4)	(9·1)	(0·5)	(0·1)
3. Newstead	0·3	(3·5)	(3·8)	(5·8)	(3·6)	(8·9)
4. Linby	(5·1)	(4·3)	(6·4)	(4·4)	1·6	(0·4)
5. Gedling	(1·2)	(2·9)	(5·2)	(1·3)	3·5	2·0
6. Bentinck	0·7	1·3	0·0	(3·5)	(5·9)	(3·5)
7. Annesley	0·6	1·5	0·8	(1·7)	(5·6)	(3·1)
8. Hucknall	4·4	5·4	0·1	1·0	(6·2)	(4·0)
9. Calverton	1·9	5·4	4·4	8·6	6·4	1·5
10. Pye Hill	6·7	6·3	3·3	6·4	4·1	4·7
11. Cotgrave	1·3	1·9	1·5	2·0	4·2	3·4

Source: The NCB.

APPENDIX 3.6(*j*)

(referred to in paragraph 3.31)

NCB deep mines

Colliery operating surplus/(loss) 1976–77 to 1981–82—(10) South Midlands Area (17 collieries)

					£ per tonne	
Colliery	1976–77	1977–78	1978–79	1979–80	1980–81	1981–82
1. Snowdown	(22·8)	(26·7)	(29·2)	(25·7)	(51·5)	(68·6)
2. Betteshanger	(3·9)	(14·6)	(7·4)	(6·1)	(10·5)	(11·0)
3. Snibston	(7·6)	(8·9)	(14·6)	(26·6)	(23·9)	(19·7)
4. Donisthorpe	(3·0)	(1·7)	(1·7)	(0·4)	(10·3)	(3·6)
5. Birch Coppice	0·1	(0·4)	(1·8)	(3·4)	(0·2)	(4·6)
6. Whitwick	(3·1)	0·0	(0·9)	(4·7)	(6·3)	(1·1)
7. Measham	0·5	(1·6)	1·0	(3·5)	(5·0)	(13·3)
8. South Leicester	(3·0)	(3·0)	0·4	(2·8)	1·0	(10·0)
9. Cadley Hill	(1·1)	0·3	1·9	(6·5)	(5·3)	(2·9)
10. Desford	1·4	1·1	0·2	(2·5)	(5·4)	(12·3)
11. Baddesley	(10·4)	1·6	0·3	(9·1)	0·9	(4·9)
12. Coventry	2·5	(7·7)	(15·3)	3·3	(11·7)	4·8
13. Tilmanstone	2·1	0·6	1·1	0·8	(16·1)	(27·0)
14. Rawdon	1·3	1·8	1·7	5·0	3·0	(3·3)
15. Ellistown	3·4	4·2	3·9	6·4	5·5	1·6
16. Daw Mill	8·5	10·3	10·4	10·8	6·3	12·5
17. Bagworth	5·2	5·1	4·2	5·5	9·9	8·7

Source: The NCB.

APPENDIX 3.6(*k*)
(referred to in paragraph 3.31)

NCB deep mines

Colliery operating surplus/(loss) 1976–77 to 1981–82—(11) Western Area (21 collieries)

£ per tonne

Colliery	1976–77	1977–78	1978–79	1979–80	1980–81	1981–82
1. Bold	(0·9)	(4·9)	(0·8)	(1·9)	(6·5)	(24·5)
2. Wolstanton	(5·1)	(2·2)	(22·6)	(14·4)	(7·6)	(13·3)
3. Bickershaw	(4·7)	(9·4)	(6·8)	(0·7)	(1·8)	(11·2)
4. Sutton Manor	(9·8)	(10·3)	(9·0)	(6·8)	(15·9)	(8·5)
5. Agecroft	(14·1)	(8·9)	(1·5)	(1·7)	(4·9)	(5·8)
6. Littleton	(0·6)	(1·7)	(4·0)	(2·9)	(8·3)	(3·8)
7. Victoria	1·6	(19·0)	(14·8)	(9·8)	(8·3)	(24·2)
8. Cronton	(4·9)	(2·6)	(5·2)	(14·4)	0·8	(12·5)
9. West Cannock	(15·7)	(3·5)	(0·9)	0·4	(8·6)	(13·2)
10. Haig	(14·8)	(14·5)	(16·7)	(13·2)	(3·0)	4·1
11. Golborne	(4·9)	(1·8)	(4·7)	(2·3)	(1·8)	1·4
12. Holditch	9·2	9·7	(17·6)	(53·3)	(12·3)	(11·6)
13. Bersham	(6·9)	0·6	4·0	(2·2)	(1·2)	(15·3)
14. Parsonage	(3·0)	(4·0)	(10·9)	(20·7)	0·9	3·7
15. Hapton Valley	(1·9)	(0·3)	0·7	(1·6)	(6·1)	12·0
16. Parkside	(5·4)	(5·6)	(0·8)	0·9	2·0	3·8
17. Hem Heath	0·7	(3·6)	(1·6)	0·5	2·3	3·7
18. Florence	3·8	1·2	(3·1)	3·0	(0·7)	7·0
19. Lea Hall	2·5	2·7	0·5	2·5	1·1	(7·4)
20. Silverdale	5·7	6·8	6·5	4·8	2·7	(0·0)
21. Point of Ayr	0·3	(1·1)	4·6	6·5	3·3	5·9

Source: The NCB.

52

(referred to in paragraph 3.31)

NCB deep mines

Colliery operating surplus/(loss) 1976–77 to 1981–82—(12) South Wales Area (33 collieries)

£ per tonne

Colliery	1976–77	1977–78	1978–79	1979–80	1980–81	1981–82
1. Treforgan	(5·4)	(3·1)	(3·3)	(20·0)	(47·2)	(104·8)
2. Tymaur/Lewis Merthyr	(7·0)	(6·4)	(4·7)	(8·5)	(20·3)	(83·9)
3. Abertillery	(2·2)	(3·9)	(5·3)	(12·3)	(31·7)	(71·0)
4. Wyndham/Western	(0·3)	(4·5)	(7·3)	(27·5)	(74·8)	(45·4)
5. Cynheidre	(31·2)	(18·4)	(18·6)	(31·3)	(25·0)	(24·1)
6. Penrikyber	(8·1)	(16·5)	(7·2)	(5·3)	(16·2)	(33·8)
7. Aberpergwm	(16·5)	(14·5)	(17·7)	(43·9)	(45·6)	(24·4)
8. Mardy	(9·9)	(23·0)	(14·1)	(15·7)	(6·8)	(24·6)
9. Abernant	(16·7)	(19·3)	(15·5)	(2·9)	(19·7)	(20·8)
10. Blaengwrach	(5·0)	(10·0)	(16·0)	(27·5)	(78·8)	(14·3)
11. Celynen South	(1·2)	(4·6)	(21·1)	(10·8)	(24·2)	(22·5)
12. Brynlliw	(3·9)	(6·2)	(9·7)	(15·9)	(27·6)	(19·8)
13. Celynen North	(14·4)	(13·3)	(5·1)	(7·6)	(28·7)	(15·3)
14. St Johns	(2·2)	(2·3)	(4·6)	(8·4)	(11·0)	(20·6)
15. Six Bells	(16·8)	(13·8)	(26·9)	(17·6)	(14·6)	(10·2)
16. Penallta	(4·6)	(1·1)	(0·4)	(5·6)	(3·7)	(1·3)
17. Tower	0·4	(6·9)	(15·8)	(3·4)	(25·2)	(33·2)
18. Bedwas	5·3	(0·6)	(14·8)	(22·4)	(34·6)	(39·4)
19. Garw	(6·5)	(2·6)	1·8	(5·3)	(16·8)	(31·0)
20. Blaenserchan	(18·4)	(7·4)	2·3	(28·8)	(16·6)	(28·0)
21. L Wind/Abercynon	(6·9)	0·5	(1·8)	(1·2)	(8·7)	(15·8)
22. Britannia	2·3	(16·2)	(1·8)	(10·3)	(26·4)	(19·3)
23. Cwm/Coedely	(0·3)	(0·4)	(2·1)	7·7	(4·9)	(5·0)
24. Merthyr Vale	(0·9)	(3·6)	(1·3)	1·5	(4·0)	(10·2)
25. Nantgarw	(6·4)	(10·2)	7·3	2·3	(14·3)	(42·5)
26. Trelewis	0·9	1·6	(0·8)	(5·8)	(25·5)	(12·9)
27. Blaenant	(3·6)	3·7	3·5	(2·4)	(0·5)	(4·9)
28. Oakdale	9·8	5·1	2·6	(12·2)	(14·5)	(30·7)
29. Markham	6·7	7·0	4·2	(1·5)	(3·9)	(26·2)
30. Taff Merthyr	(7·0)	(9·4)	2·2	6·1	4·3	(2·2)
31. Marine	5·7	1·3	3·2	(8·7)	5·3	(3·5)
32. Betws New Mine			(2·2)	(2·1)	10·0	10·5
33. Deep Navigation	4·1	3·3	(0·6)	1·2	7·0	5·4

Source: The NCB.

NCB—relationship between unit operating costs for collieries and saleable output and OMS 1981–82

Number of collieries

Operating costs (£/te)

	Under £40	£40–£50	Over £50	Total no of collieries
Output ('000 tonnes)				
Under 300	8	12	43	63
300–600	36	19	13	68
600–900	29	11	—	40
Over 900	23	4	—	27
	96	46	56	198
OMS (tonnes)				
Under 2·0	—	16	54	70
2·0–2·5	23	28	2	53
2·5–3·0	25	1		26
Over 3·0	48	1	—	49
	96	46	56	198

Source: MMC from NCB information.

Excludes two collieries that ceased production during year.

NCB—relationship between unit operating surplus/(loss) for collieries and saleable output and OMS 1981–82

Number of collieries

Operating surplus/(loss) (£/te)

	Operating surplus	Operating losses up to £10	Operating losses over £10	Total no of collieries
Output ('000 tonnes)				
Under 300	2	12	49	63
300–600	20	30	18	68
600–900	18	20	2	40
Over 900	17	9	1	27
	57	71	70	198
OMS (tonnes)				
Under 2·0	—	11	59	70
2·0–2·5	7	37	9	53
2·5–3·0	10	15	1	26
Over 3·0	40	8	1	49
	57	71	70	198

Source: MMC from NCB information.

Excludes two collieries that ceased production during year.

(referred to in paragraph 3.33)

National Coal Board

Profit and loss account summary
Monthly presentation
Run no 2

Accountable officials
Operating Manager
Finance Department

Collieries
weeks ended

Description		Actual results		Better ( ) worse (—) than:—		Cumulative last year
		Month	Cumulative	Current month	Cumulative to date	
1 (a) Saleable o/put	tnes					
(b) Disposals	tnes					
(c) Stock change	tnes					
(d) Stock at end	tnes					
2 Average manpower						
3 Man-shift worked						
(a) total face						
(b) overall						
4 (I) OMS						
(a) total face	tnes					
(b) overall	tnes					
4 (II) EMS	£					
(a) total face	£					
(b) overall	£					

	Amount £'000	Per tne £	Amount £'000	Per tne £	Amount £'000	Per tne £	Amount £'000	Per tne £
5 Proceeds								
(a) disposals								
(b) stock change								
(c) saleable								
(d) stocking provs								
(e) service charges								
(f) sub-total								
(g) sundry sales								
(h) net proceeds								
Colliery costs								
6 Wages								
7 Wages charges								
8 Materials								
9 Repairs								
10 Mining contract work								
11 Power heat and light								
12 Plant hire								
13 Salaries & rel exps								
14 Other colliery exps								
15 Depreciation								
16 Gross social costs								
17 Area overheads and services								
18 HQ overheads and services								
19 Total costs								
20 Operating profit/loss								

Source: The NCB.

APPENDIX 3.10

(referred to in paragraph 3.34)

Deep mines—movements in unit operating costs 1972–73 to 1981–82 (1976–77=100)

Year ended March	1972–73	1973–74	1974–75	1975–76	1976–77	1977–78	1978–79	1979–80	1980–81	1981–82
Operating costs										
Wages	45	54	70	90	100	111	136	155	185	198
Wages charges	28	47	54	84	100	115	122	141	164	191
Materials and repairs	37	49	62	83	100	121	130	146	170	181
Power, heat and light	37	46	62	83	100	118	130	146	180	206
Salaries and related expenses	45	60	66	82	100	113	121	142	179	206
Other colliery expenses	40	59	68	79	100	120	137	214	250	340
Overheads and services	42	54	65	82	100	118	129	148	177	200
Depreciation	61	55	46	82	100	118	131	184	235	293
Total costs	40	52	63	85	100	116	131	154	183	207
Gross social costs (included above)	88	92	80	88	100	112	124	132	200	456
Total costs, excluding gross social costs	39	51	63	85	100	116	131	155	183	204
Wholesale Price Index	51	56	71	86	100	117	127	146	167	184
Retail Price Index	53	59	69	87	100	114	123	143	166	185
Percentage increase in RPI year on year	—	11	17	26	15	14	8	16	16	11

Source: The NCB.

(referred to in paragraph 3.72)

NCB deep mines—Area relaxations 1980–81

Aggregated Area output

Area	Aggregated colliery budgets before relaxation (m tonnes)	Approved Area budget (m tonnes)	Relaxation (m tonnes)	%
Doncaster	8·5	7·7	0·8	9·5
South Yorkshire	8·7	7·9	0·8	9·1
North Derbyshire	8·4	7·7	0·7	7·9
Scottish	8·7	8·1	0·6	7·4
South Nottinghamshire	9·4	8·8	0·6	6·7
North Yorkshire	9·1	8·5	0·6	6·3
South Midlands	9·3	8·8	0·5	6·0
North Nottinghamshire	12·7	12·0	0·7	5·2
Western	11·5	11·0	0·5	4·8
Barnsley	8·4	8·1	0·3	3·6
North-East	13·8	13·5	0·3	1·9
South Wales	7·5	7·4	0·1	1·3
National	116·0	109·5	6·5	5·6

Source: The NCB.

NCB deep mines—Area relaxations 1980-81

	Aggregated surplus/(loss)		£ million
	Aggregated colliery	*Approved*	
Area	*budgets before*	*Area budget*	*Relaxation*
	relaxation		
Doncaster	17·5	(10·7)	(28·2)
South Yorkshire	33·1	(0·1)	(33·2)
North Derbyshire	39·1	15·5	(23·6)
Scottish	(23·3)	(42·0)	(18·7)
South Nottinghamshire	13·6	(5·5)	(19·1)
North Yorkshire	8·0	(10·9)	(18·9)
South Midlands	10·8	(12·1)	(22·9)
North Nottinghamshire	89·8	66·0	(23·8)
Western	(12·3)	(33·6)	(21·3)
Barnsley	(7·9)	(17·3)	(9·4)
North-East	(49·5)	(61·8)	(12·3)
South Wales	(82·7)	(99·5)	(16·8)
National	36·2	(212·0)	(248·2)

Source: The NCB.

Note: Aggregated colliery budgets before relaxations have been adjusted as indicated in final paragraph of Appendix 3.12.

National Coal Board

Area budget relaxations

It is a principle of the NCB system of accountability and management by objectives that the Area Director is formally accountable to the Board for the achievement of the key budget factors set, in agreement with him, for the Area as a whole. Within this framework, the Area Director has considerable discretion in the management of the Area's affairs; this discretion extends to the approach which the Area Director adopts to the application of relaxations to colliery budgets in preparation of the Area budget. Although the Accountability Committee will take up with the Area Director any aspect of a proposed budget relaxation which appears unreasonable in the light of the Area Director's general approach and the particular circumstance, they will only exceptionally seek to change this general approach, which is the Area Director's view as to what is most appropriate in his particular circumstances. As a result, variations in relaxations between one Area and another will arise not only from variations in physical circumstances but also from variations in management style.

In general, the factors affecting the size of the relaxations applied will be:

(a) the degree of geological risk assessed in the light of previous experience and of the details of the action programmes underlying colliery budgets; this will sometimes affect cost relaxations in addition to the output relaxation;

(b) the likely incidence of localised disputes, again assessed in the light of experience;

(c) approach to allowing for the effects of major breakdowns; it may be more practicable to take account of these at Area level where the Area is comprised largely of small pits working small numbers of faces, where the incidence of major breakdowns at a particular pit is statistically likely to be uneven, whereas in an Area made up of large pits operating large numbers of faces provision can more realistically be made in colliery budgets; and

(d) the Area Director's motivational approach; some Area Directors set individual colliery budgets which they regard as readily attainable, whereas others set colliery budgets at a more demanding level (in terms of output or costs or both) as an incentive to improved performance.

In general, the output relaxation will account for very much the largest part of the financial relaxation, with cost heading (and occasionally proceeds) relaxation accounting for the remainder.

Special factors may also affect an Area's relaxation in particular years. These could include a Board requirement to secure a further general improvement in financial performance, made at a late stage in the budgeting process; the Area Director might consider that this could be achieved by general pressure on cost control, and therefore decide to take account of this requirement by reduction of the financial relaxation rather than by adjustment of colliery budgets.

One particular factor also contributes to the difference between aggregated colliery revenue budgets and the Area revenue budget, although it does not constitute a relaxation in the same sense as the output, costs, etc relaxations. This is the amount allowed for stocking provisions held at Area level and not allocated to collieries. In 1980–81, a further factor affected the comparison between aggregate colliery revenue budgets and the Area revenue budget in some Areas; Area revenue budgets were amended to take account of the January 1981 pay/price increases, but it was left to Area Directors' discretion as to whether they would revise individual colliery budgets to take account of this, or accommodate the adjustment within the Area relaxation. The aggregated colliery budgets shown before relaxations in Appendix 11(b) have been adjusted to remove the effect of these two factors and thus to show the true relaxation when compared with the Area budget.

Source: The NCB.

NCB deep mines

Comparison of actual results with budget 1976–77 to 1981–82
(Variance shown as (+) better/(−) worse than budget)

Year ended March	1976–77			1977–78			1978–79			1979–80			1980–81			1981–82		
	Budget	Actual	Variance %	Budget	Actual	Variance %	Budget	Actual	Variance %	Budget	Actual	Variance %	Budget	Actual	Variance %	Budget	Actual	Variance %
Saleable output (m tonnes)	116·0	108·3	(−)6·7	106·1	106·1	—	116·3	107·6	(−)7·5	108·4	109·0	(+)0·5	109·5	109·4	(−)0·1	107·4	108·0	(+)0·5
Overall OMS (tonnes)	2·36	2·21	(−)6·4	2·18	2·19	(+)0·5	2·41	2·24	(−)7·3	2·33	2·27	(−)2·7	2·39	2·32	(−)2·8	2·38	2·40	(+)0·6
Average manpower	242,803	241,982	(−)0·6	240,660	240,548	—	235,861	234,889	(−)0·4	231,666	232,486	(+)0·4	230,855	229,814	(−)0·5	219,733	218,533	(−)0·5
£m																		
Net proceeds	2,108·9	2,026·2	(−)82·7	2,270·3	2,267·2	(−)3·1	2,704·7	2,492·5	(−)212·2	2,953·1	2,992·8	(+)39·7	3,586·0	3,583·8	(−)2·2	3,841·2	3,894·2	(+)53·0
Total costs	2,153·1	2,091·4	(+)61·7	2,317·1	2,334·7	(−)17·6	2,765·1	2,732·4	(+)32·7	3,179·7	3,231·4	(−)51·7	3,798·1	3,825·8	(−)27·7	4,225·3	4,205·1	(+)20·2
Operating surplus/(loss) (before interest)	(44·2)	(65·2)	(−)21·0	(46·8)	(67·5)	(−)20·7	(60·4)	(239·9)	(−)179·5	(226·6)	(238·6)	(−)12·0	(212·1)	(242·0)	(−)29·9	(384·1)	(310·9)	(+)73·2
£/te																		
Net proceeds	18·17	18·72	(+)0·55	21·40	21·37	(−)0·03	23·25	23·17	(−)0·08	27·23	27·45	(+)0·22	32·75	32·76	(+)0·01	35·75	36·07	(+)0·32
(variance as a percentage of budgeted net proceeds per tonne)			+3·0 %			−0·1 %			+0·3 %			+0·8 %			— %			+0·9 %
Operating costs £/te																		
Wages and wages charge	8·88	9·44	(−)0·56	10·46	10·67	(−)0·21	11·49	12·55	(−)1·06	14·17	14·46	(−)0·29	16·68	17·00	(−)0·32	18·29	18·17	(+)0·12
Other operating costs	9·45	9·63	(−)0·18	11·09	11·06	(+)0·03	12·03	12·54	(−)0·51	14·79	14·85	(−)0·06	17·51	17·47	(+)0·04	20·11	19·63	(+)0·48
Social costs	0·22	0·25	(−)0·03	0·29	0·28	(+)0·01	0·25	0·31	(−)0·06	0·36	0·33	(+)0·03	0·50	0·50	—	0·93	1·15	(−)0·22
Total costs £/te	18·55	19·32	(−)0·77	21·84	22·01	(−)0·17	23·77	25·40	(−)1·63	29·32	29·64	(−)0·32	34·69	34·97	(−)0·28	39·33	38·95	(+)0·38
(Variance as a percentage of budgeted total costs per tonne)			−4·2 %			−0·8 %			−6·9 %			−1·1 %			−0·8 %			+1·0 %
Operating surplus/(loss) (before interest) (£/te)	(0·38)	(0·60)	(−)0·22	(0·44)	(0·64)	(−)0·20	(0·52)	(2·23)	(−)1·71	(2·09)	(2·19)	(−)0·10	(1·94)	(2·21)	(−)0·27	(3·58)	(2·88)	(+)0·70

Source: The NCB.

Note: Budgeted results are those set Area Directors as adjusted for subsequent coal price increases and wage/salary awards.

(referred to in paragraph 3.88)

NCB—mining capital expenditure 1974–75 to 1981–82
(average 1981–82 prices)

Year ended March	New mines	Major projects	Other	£ million Total
1974–75	5	56	224	285
1975–76	14	102	315	431
1976–77	19	140	301	460
1977–78	36	171	294	501
1978–79	62	184	367	613
1979–80	86	210	447	743
1980–81	125	224	430	779
1981–82	150	229	343	722

Source: The NCB.

NCB—deep mines capital expenditure by Area 1974–75 to 1981–82 (average 1981–82 prices)

Area	New mines	Major projects	Other	Total £ million	Existing collieries with major investment costing over £1 million	
					Number of collieries	Number of projects
North Yorkshire	388	151	191	730	5	5
Barnsley	34	185	189	408	9	11
Western	2	135	268	405	12	14
North Nottinghamshire	—	129	268	397	11	26
North-East	—	104	270	374	9	15
Doncaster	24	117	212	353	9	16
South Wales	33	97	186	316	14	16
South Midlands	1	82	227	310	8	8
South Yorkshire	—	103	177	280	12	16
South Nottinghamshire	16	49	207	272	5	6
North Derbyshire	—	94	150	244	6	13
Scottish	—	65	135	200	4	6

Source: The NCB.

APPENDIX 3.16
(referred to in paragraph 3.100)

NCB and subsidiaries

Source and application of funds and financing requirements 1972–73 to 1981–82

£ million

Year ended March	1972–73	1973–74	1974–75	1975–76	1976–77	1977–78	1978–79	1979–80	1980–81	1981–82
Capital requirements										
Fixed assets	89	80	143	162	274	341	464	635	756	736
Deferred interest					2	9	14	20	41	58
Investment in associated companies and partnerships	(1)	(26)	2		4	1	3	6	10	18
Stocks of products and stores	44	(81)	23	220	50	111	171	(3)	358	95
Debtors, creditors etc	43		(115)	(55)	36	(90)	(127)	(90)	(419)	277
	175	(27)	53	327	366	372	525	568	746	1,184

Internal resources/(requirements)

Trading profit/(loss)*	(55)	(229)	(32)	25	51	33	(53)	(66)	(56)	(234)
Interest	(44)	(32)	(36)	(52)	(78)	(87)	(138)	(185)	(256)	(341)
Depreciation	78	53	59	81	93	105	120	165	210	261
Other	8	12	8	13	5	6	9	10	8	21
	(13)	(196)	(1)	67	71	57	(62)	(76)	(94)	(293)
External finance requirement	188	169	54	260	295	315	587	644	840	1,477
Financed by:										
Government grants—social	15	21	22	32	43	51	54	62	79	120
operating, regional and deficit	–	109	46	–	11	24	118	189	175	455
	15	130	68	32	54	75	172	251	254	575
Borrowings	173	39	(14)	228	241	240	415	393	586	902
	188	169	54	260	295	315	587	644	840	1,477

Source: The NCB.

*Trading profit/(loss) includes profit on realisation of fixed assets, minority interests, taxation etc and is before government grants.

67

NCB and subsidiaries

Capital structure 1972–73 to 1981–82

£ million

Year ended March (Historic cost basis)	1973*	1974	1975	1976	1977	1978†	1979	1980	1981	1982
Assets employed										
Plant, machinery and equipment	205·3	216·0	259·4	347·6	470·0	677·2	880·4	1,111·1	1,358·5	1,526·4
Mines and surface works	66·6	66·9	78·2	110·7	155·3	226·8	343·7	543·7	818·2	1,104·3
Other fixed assets	97·6	100·8	121·8	68·8	75·6	96·8	111·5	140·8	156·5	157·0
Other	103·2	129·4	39·8	205·5	301·9	335·7	397·7	332·5	322·4	765·0
Total	472·7	513·1	499·2	732·6	1,002·8	1,336·5	1,733·3	2,128·1	2,655·6	3,552·7
Financed by										
Loans*	441·5	480·0	465·7	693·5	935·1	1,175·1	1,590·3	1,983·5	2,569·0	3,470·5
Other	31·2	33·1	33·5	39·1	67·7	161·4	143·0	144·6	86·6	82·2
Total	472·7	513·1	499·2	732·6	1,002·8	1,336·5	1,733·3	2,128·1	2,655·6	3,552·7
Loans as a percentage of total assets employed	93%	94%	93%	95%	93%	88%	92%	93%	97%	98%

Source: NCB published accounts.

*There was a capital reconstruction at March 1973 and fixed assets were written down by £275 million and the accumulated revenue deficit of £174·6 million written off. A total amount of £449·6 million was extinguished from Loans from the Secretary of State, leaving a balance of £413 million consolidated in accordance with the Coal Industry Act 1973 bearing interest at 5·5 per cent per annum and repayable over a term of 20 years.

†At the time of the capital reconstruction in 1973 provision was made to write down the assets at some collieries which were expected to have a short life. In the changed circumstances of the industry some of these collieries were considered to have further years of operation and the value of the relevant assets was reinstated. The net book value of colliery assets at March 1978 was increased by £68 million and a corresponding amount transferred to reserves.

The influence of ageing of pits on productivity

1. The main asset of the coal industry is the non-renewable resource represented by the coal seams upon which the production units, the pits, are based. As the seams are penetrated and mineral is extracted the effectiveness of the production units shows a potential for steady decline.

2. Whereas in many other industries the effectiveness of an existing production unit can be maintained by a constant steady stream of capital and management effort, in mining an increasing level of effort is required in existing units as the resources are depleted. Effectiveness over the industry as a whole can be fully restored by investment in new rather than existing capacity but this will occur in discrete tranches only at significant intervals.

3. The reasons for this inherent decline in productivity in existing mines are two-fold. First, coal seams are not homogeneous, they vary from location to location in quality, in thickness and in the geological conditions such as faults, and inclusion of foreign matter. In so far as other factors allow when new mines are developed on a seam their location, and in particular the shaft or drift, is chosen to give easy access to the best working areas. Secondly, as the working faces advance during extraction their distance from the shaft or drift bottom increases. This factor would, however, be less important in a mine where all or a significant proportion of faces were worked in the total retreat mode of operation. These two natural effects result in a number of adverse trends:

   (a) Since the tendency is for the best areas to be worked first the working quality of the faces tends to reduce:

      (i) thinner seams;

      (ii) greater proportion of dirt in the exracted mineral; and

      (iii) more severe gradients.

   (b) Interaction with exhausted workings in other seams, especially in terms of roof stability, increases.

   (c) A greater proportion of man-shift time is spent travelling to the face.

   (d) A greater proportion of manpower is required elsewhere below ground to maintain the increasing length of road and to supervise the coal and materials conveyance system.

   (e) If quality deteriorates as the mine ages then coal preparation and quality enhancement on the surface becomes more extensive.

   The first two factors affect productivity by reducing the extraction rate of useful product at the face, the last three factors affect productivity by increasing the total need for manpower at constant output.

4. Figure 1 shows the average percentage vend for the NCB output over the period 1970–71 to 1980–81. The proportion of saleable product has reduced by about 2 per cent over the period, which is equivalent to a productivity reduction at the face, in terms of OMS, of about 2·5 per cent.

FIGURE 1

National trend in percentage vend over the period 1970–71 to 1981–82

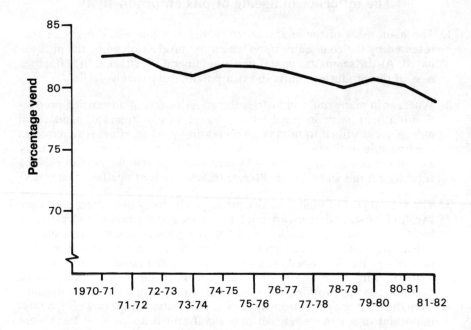

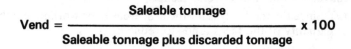

$$\text{Vend} = \frac{\text{Saleable tonnage}}{\text{Saleable tonnage plus discarded tonnage}} \times 100$$

Source: MMC from NCB information.

5. Figure 2 shows the trend in average round trip distance from the shaft bottom to the working faces and back again over the period 1976–77 to 1980–81. The average distance to the face has increased by about 17 per cent, which approximately corresponds to an increase in travel time under constant conditions of between 10 and 15 minutes or a reduction in productive time at the face of about 5 per cent which will be directly reflected in face OMS.

6. Over the ten years 1970–71 to 1980–81 the combination of the trend in vend and travelling time together represent an inherent maximum reduction in overall OMS of between 5 and 8 per cent, depending on the detail of the counter-measures adopted by management. However, greater distance to the face results in increased roadway repairs, extended coal and materials transport system requiring operation and maintenance, and giving increased probability of breakdown and delay. Eight per cent is, therefore, probably an under-estimate of the inherent decline.

7. Thus in order just to maintain productivity of saleable product at a constant level, the NCB must improve efficiency in existing capacity by at least 0·5 to 0·75 per cent each year. To show an observable real gain in productivity will require additional action including capital expenditure. There may also be an additional adverse factor which is difficult to quantify in cases where geological conditions become less favourable with age.

8. The investigation of productivity performance requires the evaluation of two elements, firstly the inherent rate of decline resulting from the ageing of the pits and secondly the contribution to improvement brought about by the various management actions. The net effect of the two is evident and can be measured, but it may not be feasible to separate the two components or the relative contributions from the various actions. A net negative trend would not necessarily indicate management failure or reducing management effort, but may simply indicate that the best seams have been worked out; the rate of development of mining technology and the rate of introduction of replacement or new capacity are not sufficient to compensate.

FIGURE 2

Trend in national average inbye plus outbuy distance on major longwall faces

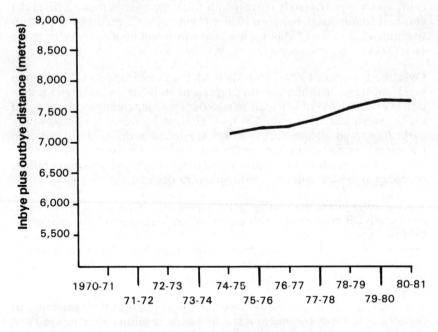

(Average, half year ending)

Note: Inbye and outbye distances are the distance from shaftbottom to the production face, and the distance from the production face back to the shaftbottom respectively.

Source: MMC from NCB information.

Improvement in manpower productivity 1969–70 to 1981–82

1. The improvement in manpower productivity nationally of about 9 per cent in overall revenue OMS from 1969–70 to 1981–82, has resulted from the following factors:

    (*a*) redistribution of production geographically;

    (*b*) improved use of manpower (including the effect of the incentive scheme); and

    (*c*) improved machine systems resulting in better extraction rates at the face.

2. *Distribution of OMS and output between faces, pits and Areas.*
    For reasons which are mainly beyond the direct control of management the various production units, ie the faces and pits, have widely differing values of OMS. One strategy for increasing the average value of OMS, and hence producing a cost reduction, is to increase the proportion of total output contributed by the high productivity units, for the NCB in terms of Area production, for an Area Director in terms of pits and for a pit manager in terms of faces.

3. Figure 1 shows the distribution of output per shift for individual faces in 1970–71, 1975–76 and 1980–81, Figure 2 shows the distribution of overall OMS for individual pits over the same periods and Figure 3 shows the percentage of total output for each Area ranked by OMS again over the same periods.

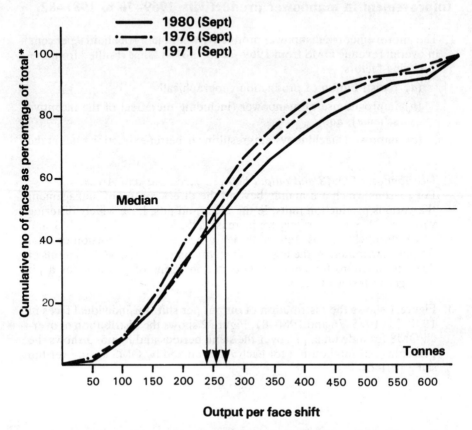

FIGURE 1

Cumulative graph showing the percentage of faces with output per face shift less than a given value for September 1971, 1976, 1980.

*Figure represents the cumulative number of faces as a percentage of total with output per face shift less than the value indicated on the horizontal scale.

Source: MMC from NCB information.

FIGURE 2

Cumulative graph showing the percentage of collieries with overall revenue OMS less than a
given value for 1970–71, 1975–76, 1980–81

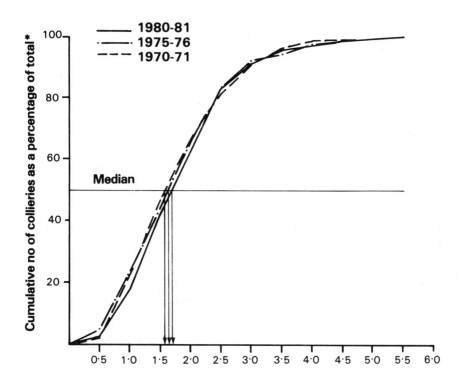

Overall revenue OMS (saleable tonnes/man-shift)

*Figure represents the cumulative number of collieries as a percentage of
total with overall revenue OMS less than the value indicated on the
horizontal scale.

Source: MMC from NCB information.

FIGURE 3

Cumulative percentage of saleable output per year for the twelve NCB Areas in ascending order of overall revenue OMS for 1970-71, 1975-76, 1980-81

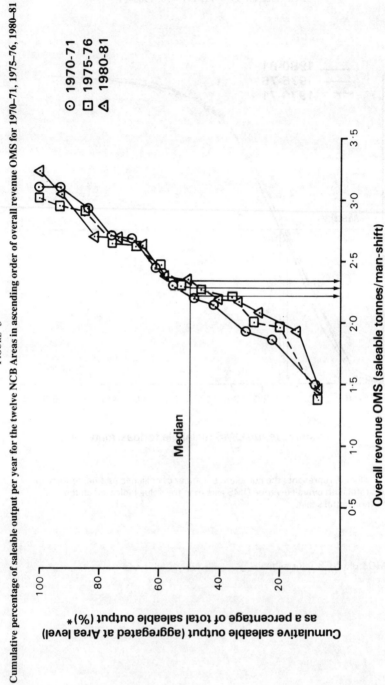

⊙ 1970-71
□ 1975-76
△ 1980-81

Overall revenue OMS (saleable tonnes/man-shift)

Cumulative saleable output (aggregated at Area level)
as a percentage of total saleable output (%)*

*Figure represents the cumulated output by Area as a percentage of total saleable output with average Area overall revenue OMS less than the value indicated on the horizontal scale.

Source: MMC from NCB information.

76

4. The analysis shows that the Area with the highest contribution to output ranks low in the order of OMS. However, the evidence is that between 1970–71 and 1980–81 output between the Areas has been adjusted to favour those with higher OMS. In 1970–71 the top six Areas produced 44 per cent of output whereas in 1980–81 they produced 49 per cent output and in 1981–82 they produced 51 per cent. They have also had some success with the reduction of the proportion of pits with OMS less than two tonnes and with reducing the proportion of faces with outputs per shift less than 250 tonnes.

5. *Improved use of manpower.* Some labour productivity gains have been achieved by reducing manpower at the face and on the surface for a constant output of coal. Figure 4 shows the ratio of man-shifts worked to machine shifts worked at the face and provides some indication of the trend in the average manpower needed to work and maintain a face. The value started to reduce quite sharply in 1977–78 and appears to have been reduced by about 12 per cent in total.

FIGURE 4

Trend in face man-shifts per machine shift, 1974–75 to 1980–81

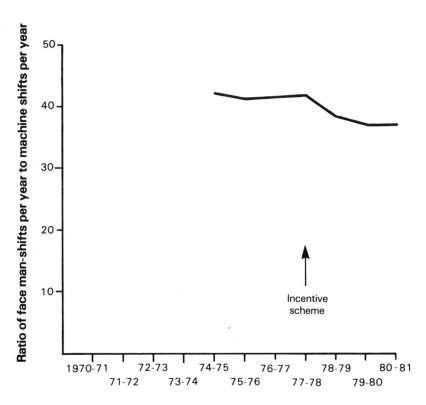

Source: MMC from NCB information.

77

6. There are two contributions to the gains in labour productivity at the face and on the surface, firstly the implementation of the incentive scheme and secondly investment in improved machinery, especially heavy duty and advanced technology mining systems at the face, and labour-saving remote control machinery at the surface. Major investment schemes such as a new drift will increase productivity on the surface and EBG by improving the clearance rate for the same manpower and even at the face in cases where production is limited by shaft capacity. Additionally surface productivity has been improved in some cases by merging pits, and taking advantage of economies of scale by using common surface facilities.

7. *Performance trends in coal extraction rates.* Figure 5 shows the trend in daily output per face over the period 1974–75 to 1980–81 which shows a dip in performance in 1976–77 since when there has been an improvement of about 18 per cent. The increase in DOF may have resulted from:

   (*a*) An increased number of shifts per day per face. Figure 6 shows the trend in the shifting index.

   (*b*) Change to retreat mining. Figure 7 shows the ratio of output for retreat faces to advancing faces. Retreat faces appear to have about 30 to 50 per cent higher face output per day. Figure 8 shows the ratio of number of retreat to advance faces. Retreat mining can be used only in particular conditions and so is not always a valid alternative.

   (*c*) An increase in the output per machine shift. Figure 5 also sets out the trend in output per machine shift, which has increased by about 8 per cent over the period 1976 to 1980.

8. *Trend in output per machine shift.* The increase in output per machine shift appears to have been achieved by a combination of factors including improved face technology and coal clearance and the introduction of the incentive scheme. Figure 9 shows the trend in volume swept per machine shift.

9. During the period under investigation the average length of face has increased and the unscheduled lost time per machine shift has been reduced. Figure 10 shows the trend in face length over the period 1970 to 1980. Table 1 shows an analysis of the trend in the times associated with the component activities, including unscheduled lost time, comprising a machine shift. The analysis was derived from the data supplied by the face delay analysis system. The procedure is to sample a small number of shifts in each Area at intervals of about three months which provides estimates correct to about ±5 per cent. The results provide an indication of a national trend, but may not be representative of any particular colliery, and are not suitable for managerial control at individual faces. The two trends in face length and lost time should have resulted in a substantial increase in the machine running time per shift. However, the analysis shown in Table 1 suggests that the expected improvement has not been achieved; indeed machine running time is currently less than it was in 1976–77.

FIGURE 5

Trend in daily output per face and output per machine shift (major longwall faces) over period 1974–75 to 1981–82

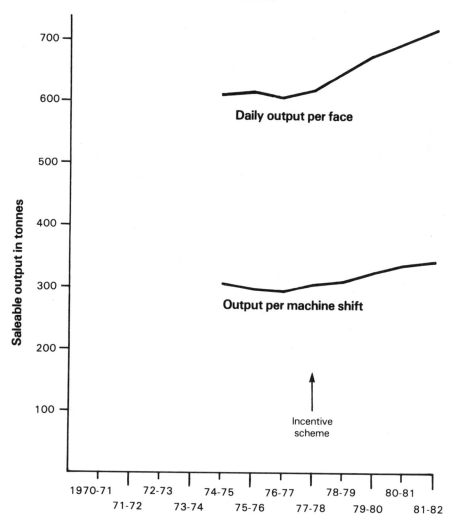

Source: MMC from NCB information.

FIGURE 6

Trend in average number of shifts per day per face (for a sample week in September) over the period 1970 to 1980

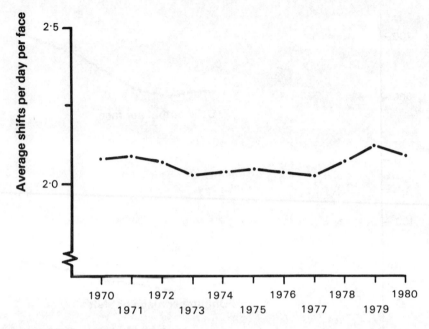

Source: MMC from NCB information.

FIGURE 7

Trend in ratio of daily output per face for retreating faces to daily output per face for advancing faces over the period 1970 to 1981 (based on a September sample)

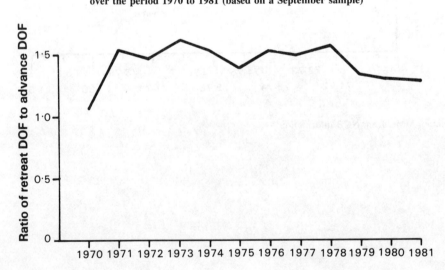

Source: MMC study.

80

FIGURE 8

Trend in the percentage of faces working in the retreat mode over the period 1970 to 1981 (based on a September sample)

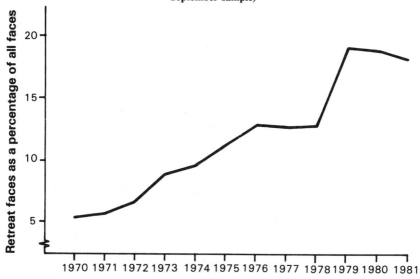

Source: MMC from NCB information.

FIGURE 9

Trend in volume swept per face shift (based on a sample week in September) over the period 1971 to 1981

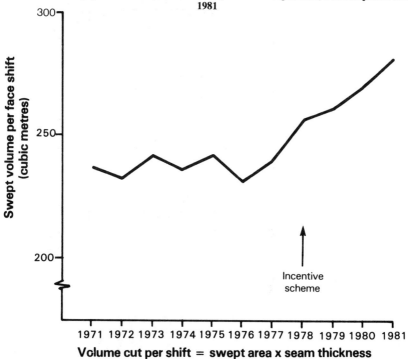

Volume cut per shift = swept area x seam thickness

Source: MMC from NCB information.

TABLE 1 **Analysis of shift time with trends in component activities over the period 1976–77 to 1981–82**

Man-shift time in minutes

| Year | Machine available time in minutes | | | Lost time | Total MAT | Other time in minutes | | | Total man-shift time |
	Machine running time	Ancillary time	Oper-ational			Prepar-ation and snap time	Travel-ling time	Total other time	
1976–77	112	29	60	116	317	28	90	118	435
1977–78	105	31	64	118	318	28	89	117	435
1978–79	100	34	64	115	313	29	93	122	435
1979–80	109	33	67	106	315	29	91	120	435
1980–81	109	33	65	108	315	29	91	120	435
1981–82	109	38	66	103	316	29	90	119	435

Source: The NCB.

82

FIGURE 10

Trend in face length for major longwall faces over the period 1970 to 1981 (based on a September sample)

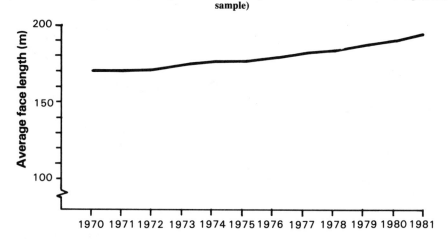

Source: MMC from NCB information.

10. Labour productivity from new mines and existing mines with major projects was significantly higher than the average in 1981–82. Overall revenue OMS averaged 4·78 tonnes for projects associated with new mines approved since the Plan for Coal was introduced and 2·62 tonnes at existing mines with completed major projects compared with the national average of 2·40 tonnes.

11. Figure 11 shows the national trend in OMS by category. Face OMS has improved by over 30 per cent in the period 1970–71 to 1981–82 and surface OMS by about 20 per cent in the same period. However, elsewhere below ground OMS on average has declined by about 11 per cent, which when taken with due account of the actual proportion of total manpower in this category significantly offsets the gains at the face and on the surface.

FIGURE 11

Trend in national average overall revenue OMS and OMS for major work categories over the periods 1969–70 to 1981–82

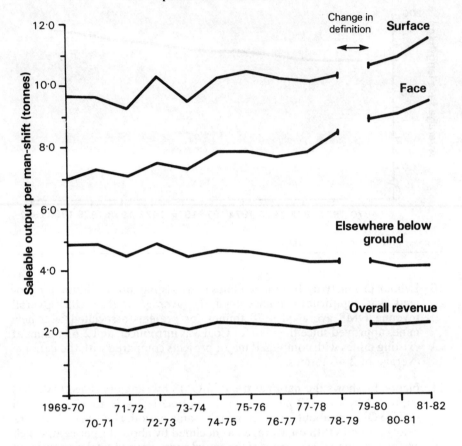

Notes: (1) After 1978–79 there is a change in definition.

(2) After 1978–79 'overall OMS' is redefined as 'overall revenue OMS'.

Source: MMC from NCB information.

APPENDIX 6.3
(referred to in paragraphs 6.40, 6.41, 6.42, 6.46 and 6.48)

A framework of performance measures

1. Most industries develop their own technical language which reflects their own specific needs. In particular the nomenclature and formulation of performance measures with which management monitor the progress of the business form an integral part of the technical language. Mining is no exception and those who are unfamiliar with the industry may have difficulty in setting the rather large variety of measures into perspective. This appendix is intended to assist the ordinary reader to an understanding of the scope of measures which are relevant to good management control, how they relate to each other and to unit cost.

2. The total unit cost of coal production may be presented in terms of three productivity indices, for labour, materials and capital, and three unit resource cost indices for the same categories. To calculate values of the productivity indices it is necessary to measure:

   (*a*) output;

   (*b*) manpower input;

   (*c*) materials input; and

   (*d*) capital input.

To diagnose the reasons for productivity variation and to plan and implement management action to improve total productivity and reduce unit cost, it is necessary to have measures of the values of factors contributing to the variations of output and manpower etc.

3. The NCB collects and processes colliery data for its management information system by means of a comprehensive statistics function. The primary data collected includes:

   (*a*) *production information* such as saleable output produced, number of machine shifts etc;

   (*b*) *manpower information* such as number of employees, number of man-shifts worked; and

   (*c*) *technical information* such as type of machine system in use, face length, seam thickness.

This is supplemented by the normal accounting data which provide production cost information such as earnings per man-shift (EMS). Some of the data, for example, output are tabulated shift by shift for each face, while other data, such as machine available time, are obtained by sampling procedures. The basic data are used to produce a number of primary and derived performance measures which are reported routinely throughout the year and summarised annually.

4. In the discussion which follows we have tried to set out a framework of the type of measures which are used in the mining industry. We represent the

85

principal measures conceptually in terms of a number of related factors in order to illustrate two aspects:

(a) the relationship between the measures and the degree to which they are interdependent; and

(b) the degree to which the performance depends on factors which are under management control or external factors.

There are a number of ways in which the relationships could be set out, and the ones we have chosen do not necessarily correspond to the procedure by which the NCB estimates the values of the measures from primary data.

5. In the rest of this appendix we discuss:

(a) annual output and associated measures;

(b) annual man-shifts;

(c) manpower productivity; and

(d) capital productivity.

Figure 1 summarises diagrammatically the framework of the discussion and the broad relationship between the range of measures. Where appropriate we indicate the areas of the conceptual framework for which the NCB has specific measures. The process of simplification inevitably brings with it a loss of precision and some omissions.

Annual output and associated measures

Output tonnage

6. The definition of output tonnage merits some consideration, should it, for example, include coal produced and put into stocks. Product stocks are an essential management device to smooth short-term variations in demand and production rates.

7. There are four main possibilities for measuring the output:

(a) include all mineral mined in the period;

(b) include all coal produced in the period of saleable quality;

(c) include all coal sold in the period; and

(d) include only that proportion of coal produced and sold in the period.

The first is more concerned with mining control and the other three more concerned with business control. The two groups are related by the vend (see paragraph 8). In terms of overall business efficiency of the organisation including the ability to match supply and demand, definition (b) may over-estimate efficiency in periods of falling demand if production and hence stocks are not reduced and the surplus is placed in stock. Definition (c) would tend to over-estimate efficiency in periods of rising demand as coal is sold from stocks. Definition (d) avoids some of these difficulties but would introduce difficulties in measuring operational productivity in individual units. The NCB uses a definition similar to (b)—saleable tonnage produced in the period.

86

FIGURE 1

The broad relationship between performance measures

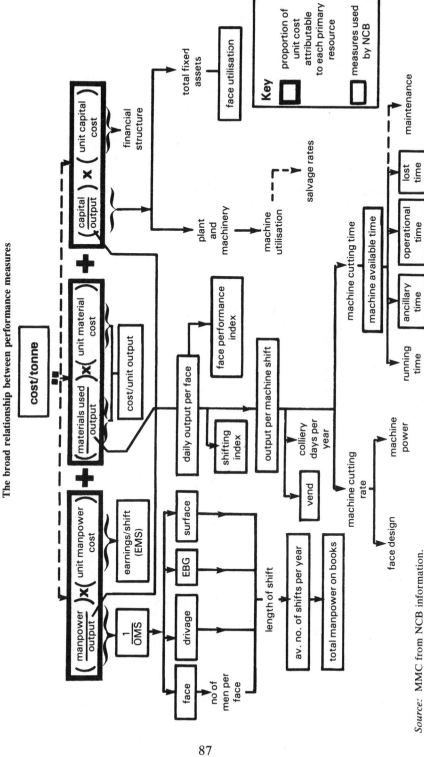

Source: MMC from NCB information.

Output associated measures

8. The total annual output of coal from deep mining may be set out conceptually in terms of a number of more fundamental factors concerned with the level of mining technology, the operational conditions at the face, and the manning policy. The analysis illustrates the large number of performance indicators that are necessary for adequate management control and the level of detail that is necessary to highlight areas which are likely to respond favourably to management action.

A: *Total annual output (tonnes/year)*

=Total daily output (tonnes) × average days worked/year.

Capital productivity will depend very much on the proportion of days in the year that each colliery is actually working. The NCB calculates the annual output directly by summing the actual daily saleable output for each day of the year.

B: *Total daily output (tonnes)*

=Volume of mineral extracted per day per face (cubic metres)
× Average number of faces worked per day
× Density of mineral (tonnes per cubic metre)
× Vend proportion.

The vend is a measure used by the NCB to indicate the proportion of useful output. It is the ratio of saleable tonnage to the sum of saleable tonnage and discarded tonnage. The NCB calculates the actual daily output directly by summing the actual saleable output from each face producing during the day.

C: *Volume of mineral extracted per day per face* (cubic metres)
=Machine traverse rate whilst cutting (metres/minutes)
× Seam height (metres)
× Depth of cut (metres)
× Cutting time per day (minutes).

The NCB calculates the actual volume of mineral extracted on a face during the working day as follows:
Total face length (metres) × Seam height (metres) × Advance (metres).

9. For the past two years the NCB has used a new measure which discounts both vend and seam thickness as a measure of effort in using machines effectively. The measure used is 'square metres of face swept per 100 minutes of machine available time' (see paragraph 14). The swept area is a measure that the NCB can tabulate easily from statistics already collected, ie from face length and face advance. The relationship between volume and swept area is:

Swept area   =Machine traverse rate (metres/minutes)
       × Depth of cut (metres)
       × Cutting time (minutes)
Volume extracted =Swept area × seam height.

In Germany a similar measure is in routine use, but the units are chosen to be square metres swept per man-shift to be consistent with the more usual measure used for labour productivity which is discussed later.

10. The rate at which the machines can extract mineral depends on many factors, such as the machine system design, the horsepower available and the rate at which a man can travel through the face with the machine in a restricted working height. The potential cutting rate may be reduced by the presence of geological faults and intrusions.

D: *Machine cutting rate*
   =Traverse rate × depth of cut × seam height.

The maximum value is limited by the power available. The depth of cut is constrained by the particular design of support equipment and by legal requirements.

11. Once the standard cutting depths and traverse rate are set, one indicator of effort is the number of traverses made and an alternative equivalent measure used by the NCB is 'linear metres cut at standard strip depth per shift'. These will measure the effort in reducing the time to reset the face for the next cut and also in reducing unscheduled stoppages. The number of traverses will only be a useful measure if the depth of cut is constant and pre-set: if not, then the measure could provide spurious values if for example shallow but fast cuts were made. Also one would expect such a measure to favour short faces. For these reasons the number of traverses made is a poor control measure. The standardised measure of linear metres cut per shift helps to overcome the difficulties.

E: *Number of traverses per day*
$$=\frac{\text{Machine traverse rate} \times \text{cutting time per day}}{\text{Total face length}}$$

The NCB would estimate the number of traverses more directly by dividing the total length cut by the machine by the power loaded face length.

F: *Linear distance cut*=Number of traverses × total face length.

12. The machine cutting time per day, given a particular set of machine systems, can be influenced very much by management planning and supervision in a number of ways:

   (*a*) selection of machine system;

   (*b*) face design;

   (*c*) retreat or advance working;

   (*d*) shifting pattern;

   (*e*) incentives scheme; and

   (*f*) maintenance.

G: *Cutting time per day*
   =machine cutting time per shift × Number of shifts per day.

Cutting time is clearly a very important measure because it represents true productive time. However, it is not tabulated directly by the NCB.

H: *Machine cutting time per shift*
=Machine available time per shift
  less ancillary time
  less operational time
  less lost time.
The NCB uses the following definitions:

Machine ancillary time: The time when a machine is temporarily out of production for activities which are inherent in its operation and are planned to happen at the time and place when they happen, eg scheduled machine maintenance, preparing a shearer for cutting, pick changing.

Machine operational time: The time spent on activities other than machine running time (see below) and machine ancillary time which are inherent in the system, eg breaking large coal, shot firing.

Lost time: The delay time to a machine arising from incorrect or sub-standard work, poor organisation of the face activities, clearance systems or services eg cable handler fast, gate conveyor overloaded, ramp plate loose, abnormal geological conditions.

Machine running time: The NCB uses this term for the time that the machine is actually cutting coal. In the discussions above we have used the term machine cutting time for this. The NCB estimates the standard machine running time as follows. The average machine speed is calculated from those observed times and distances when the machine was cutting at normal depth and operating in the correct horizon. The standard running time is obtained by dividing the power loaded length over which the machine operates by the average speed.

Machine cycle time at standard consists of three parts:

  (*a*) standard machine running time per cycle;

  (*b*) standard machine ancillary time per cycle; and

  (*c*) standard machine operational time per cycle.

13. The NCB does not consider machine running time a useful measure, firstly because machines may undertake a variety of operations whilst running, such as trim cuts and horizon corrections as well as production cuts; secondly because of the number of machine designs each needing different operational procedures; and thirdly on multi-machine faces, one or more of the machines is designed to be idle for part of the cycle time. In Germany machine running time and cutting time are used to monitor utilisation.

14. Machine available time is measured routinely by the NCB. The element which can be influenced directly by management by investment is the time taken in travelling from the shaft to the face and back, whilst refreshment breaks and preparation tasks etc can be influenced by the normal management supervision and consultation procedures. As the pit ages and the seams are worked the travelling time will increase naturally. Travelling time can be decreased by capital investment in man-riders, and driving new, more direct, roads from the shaft bottom. The British Standards Institution defines machine available time as 'the proportion of a time

90

cycle during which a machine could be performing useful work'. The NCB bases its calculations on a time cycle of one man-shift.

I: *Machine available time per shift*[1]
=Length of shift
less time spent in face preparation
less meal break
less time spent travelling to and from the face
less time spent at the end of the shift putting away tools etc.

Annual man-shifts

15. In a similar manner total annual man-shifts may be set out in terms of a number of components:

A. *Total annual man-shifts*
=Number of colliery days worked per year
× Average number of shifts per day
× Average number of men per shift.
The NCB calculates annual man-shifts directly by summing the individual daily man-shifts worked in the year. For face workers in particular the analysis may be extended as follows:

B. *Average number of men per shift*
=Average number of men per face
× Average number of production faces.
The average number of shifts per day may also be represented in terms of the total men on the books:

C. *Average number of man-shifts per day*
=Total manpower on books.
× Average number of shifts per man per day.

16. Taking into account public holidays, rest days and annual holidays each man may be expected to work a standard number of shifts per year. Man-shifts may be lost as the result of accidents, sickness, voluntary absence, training or industrial disputes etc. Additional shifts may be worked through overtime.

17. Normally the number of men employed is such that with the expected absence rates each shift can be manned to planned levels. If absence rates change without a compensatory change in the total workforce then there may well be a decline in productivity. If more men than needed turn up for a shift the additional men will be paid but may be given work of a lower priority which does not increase coal production; if too few men turn up, some teams may be undermanned and less viable.

---

[1] This is a rather particular use of the term by the NCB. Other operators in non-British mining industries reserve it for measuring the time the machine itself is available for work, and not the time that the labour is available to work the machine.

Manpower productivity

18. Manpower productivity is commonly monitored by a measure similar to the following:

$$\text{Manpower productivity} = \frac{\text{Output achieved in the period}}{\text{Manpower units used in period}}$$

The choice of suitable definition and units for output would depend upon the intended use of the measure and the considerations discussed in paragraph 7. Manpower units are commonly measured in terms of number of men, shifts worked or hours worked.

19. The NCB has developed a comprehensive set of labour productivity measures in terms of 'saleable output per man-shift' (OMS). An OMS productivity measure is defined by the NCB for different categories of work:

(1) Major longwall mechanised face OMS $= \dfrac{\text{MLMF saleable output}}{\text{Man-shifts on MLMF (incl overtime)}}$

(2) Production OMS $= \dfrac{\text{Production saleable output}}{\text{Production man-shifts}}$

(3) Other underground OMS $= \dfrac{\text{Total revenue saleable output (incl lifted slurry)}}{\text{Development \& underground services man-shifts}}$

(4) All underground OMS $= \dfrac{\text{Total revenue saleable output}}{\text{All underground man-shifts}}$

(5) Surface OMS $= \dfrac{\text{Total revenue saleable output}}{\text{Surface man-shifts}}$

(6) Overall revenue OMS $= \dfrac{\text{Total revenue saleable output}}{\text{Total underground \& surface man-shifts}}$

(7) Revenue+capital OMS $= \dfrac{\text{Total revenue saleable output+ capital output}}{\text{Total underground+surface+ capital man-shifts}}$

Revenue shifts are those for which the expenditure is charged to the revenue account; capital shifts are those which are associated with capital works and expenditure on labour is capitalised. The measure is precisely defined and includes the following details:

(*a*) It includes production into stocks after preparation.

(*b*) Current make of slurry disposed of is included in output but lifted slurry is included only when sold.

(*c*) Certain shifts paid for but not worked are not included, eg training shifts or authorised attendances at training college.

The use of a number of OMS measures is an attempt to separate the contributions to total productivity changes by different categories of work.

Productivity of capital assets

20. The NCB does not calculate a measure for total capital productivity in terms of output per unit value of capital employed, but does produce routinely related measures for two classes of asset in terms of face productivity and machine productivity.

21. Face machinery is sometimes tied up in spare or standby faces. It is helpful to management to know both the utilisation of the assets (ie the proportion of the assets which are productive) and also the productivity of those assets which are contributing to production (ie the output rate per working unit). Utilisation can be estimated and monitored by measures similar to the following:

    Face utilisation

    $$= \frac{\text{Average number of producing faces per day in period}}{\text{Average number of faces equipped per day in period}}$$

    Machine utilisation

    $$= \frac{\text{Sum of machine shifts worked on producing faces in period}}{\text{Sum of potential machine shifts on all equipped faces in period}}$$

    The productivity of faces and machines which are actually producing are monitored routinely by the NCB using the following measures:

    Face productivity (daily output per face)

    $$= \frac{\text{Sum of saleable output for each face in period}}{\text{Sum of days worked for each face in period}}$$

    Machine productivity (output per machine shift)

    $$= \frac{\text{Sum of saleable output for each face}}{\text{Sum of machine shifts worked on each face}}$$

22. The NCB monitors, at regular intervals, the number of faces which are not producing in a normal week. A normal week is one in which the colliery is working for five days. The information from which to derive a face utilisation index is therefore available. A measure called the shifting index is also monitored regularly. The shifting index measures the number of machine shifts worked per face day worked. It is a measure of the time utilisation of machinery on faces which are actually producing but does not monitor utilisation with respect to potential machine shifts on all faces which are equipped and capable of production. For the assets held by the plant pool an index is produced routinely which represents the proportion of the pool stock which is currently on rent to the collieries. For a number of reasons, including plant waiting for salvage on discontinued faces, the index does not provide a measure of utilisation in terms of plant which is actively engaged in mining coal.

23. Daily output per face and the output per machine shift are related in a simple manner, as follows:

    $$\text{DOF} = \text{Output per machine shift} \times \frac{\text{Sum of machine shifts worked on each face}}{\text{Sum of days worked on each face}}$$

    $$= \text{Output/machine shift} \times \text{shifting index.}$$

93

24. The NCB considers that as a measure it prefers DOF to output per machine shift because there are difficulties in the precise definition of a machine shift, especially when multi-machine faces are used. DOF is a useful practical measure of face productivity which is easy to tabulate and monitor; but may suffer distortions because it favours faces with thick seams and with long machine available time.

The contributions of physical and management factors to productivity and cost changes

1. The Operational Research Executive of the NCB has undertaken for the Central Planning Unit a number of analyses of historic data on the production of coal from faces, collieries and Areas in an attempt to determine the relative importance of the various physical factors and the range of management actions. In this appendix we discuss the results of these analyses.

Productivity and physical factors

2. The first analysis covers the period of data for 1950 to 1975 and was concerned with an overall NCB relationship. The work suggested that nearly all of the variations in OMS could be explained by three factors:

   (*a*) the output of mechanised faces as a percentage of total;

   (*b*) the percentage of major longwall faces with powered supports; and

   (*c*) the tonnage lost in disputes.

   However, other factors were also changing at the time. There was a programme of investment in new and reconstructed pits, a reduction in total capacity, and the average size of pit doubled; in addition there was a change in the market and the regional pattern of production. A further factor which should have been significant was that the production from seams greater than 6 feet thick increased from about 7 per cent to about 30 per cent.

3. The NCB believes that results of the analysis are consistent with the other factors in the following sense. The falling demand enabled a reduction in the less productive capacity, and at the same time changes in technology at the face place a premium on thick seams and favourable geology. These two, together with considerable investment, allowed production to be concentrated on thick seams with good geological conditions.

4. The second analysis carried out in 1977 concentrated on understanding the relationship at the coal face level. The analysis suggested that about 30 per cent of the variations in OMS at a particular face could be explained by variation in rank (a measure of the physical and chemical maturity of the coal giving some indication of calorific value, workability etc), seam thickness, distance inbye, and dip, taken together and 10 per cent by the face length, 6 per cent by the regions, and 4 per cent by the type of cutting machine.

5. This analysis highlighted the importance of working with thick level seams, and the loss of productivity as the distance inbye increased. This confirmed that investment in man-riding systems should be a priority.

6. Table 1 shows a summary of the two analyses in terms of the contribution of various factors to the increase of productivity in the 1960s.

TABLE 1   **Factors affecting face productivity 1950 to 1975**

Factor	Contribution
% change in face mechanisation	30%
%change in faces with powered supports	28%
Change in length of face	13%
Change in seam thickness	19%
Change in regional distribution	10%

Source: The NCB.

7. The third analysis was undertaken with data at colliery level to obtain an understanding of the relationship between OMS and colliery characteristics. The NCB interpretation of this analysis is that:

   (*a*) drift mines have significantly higher OMS than shaft mines;

   (*b*) existing mines show modest returns to scale in terms of productivity;

   (*c*) the regional pattern of production is significant;

   (*d*) seam thickness, dirt and vend are significant; and

   (*e*) OMS reduces as the shaft to face distance increases.

8. As with all statistical analyses the confidence in the results depends on the quality of the data available, and must be interpreted in the context of the original hypotheses. The Operational Research Executive of the NCB has a high reputation and we believe that the analyses were carried out with proper professional judgment; however, the Executive suggests that the results should be regarded with caution.

Factors affecting production cost

9. The NCB has also attempted to analyse the changes in cost structure over the past five years, both in terms of policy changes and in terms of functional operations. The methodology is not fully developed and a number of assumptions and accounting conventions need to be explored. The NCB looked at five factors which were expected to influence the production cost and attempted to quantify their effects. These were:

   (*a*) closures;

   (*b*) structural changes, size of pits, balance of Area production, size of Areas;

   (*c*) price changes—levels of wages/materials etc with respect to a national price index;

   (*d*) volume changes—volume of manpower/materials per tonne of production; and

   (*e*) specific changes—changes in accounting policy and new pension schemes, etc.

96

10. Table 2 shows the results of the NCB analysis in terms of annual percentage contribution to total cost increase for each of the identified areas.

Table 2 **Factors affecting cost increase in deep-mined coal production 1975–76 to 1980–81**

Factor	Percentage Increase in total		
(a) Closures	−0·1		
(b) Change in area balance at continuing pits	−0·9		
(c) Increased production from new mines and continuing collieries	−0·6	———	
(d) Productivity increases from other sources	−0·4	−2·0	
(e) Deterioration in physical parameters	+0·3	———	
(f) Increase in wages	+2·5		
(g) Increase in wages charges	+1·2		
(h) Voluntary early retirement	+0·4		
(i) Increase in plant hire	+0·6		
(j) Increase in depreciation	+0·2	———	
(k) All other sources	+0·5	5·7	
(l) Changes in accounting*	−0·8	———	
Total		+2·9	

Source: The NCB.

*Capitalisation of drivages and superannuation deficiency.

11. The factors (a), (b), (c), (d) suggest that management have had some success in restructuring and changing the pattern of production to the high OMS units. This has apparently been more than offset over the period of analysis by the manpower related costs (f), (g), (h).

12. In 1981–82 cost did not increase, indicating a better balance between manpower and non-manpower costs. The NCB considers that this results from the maturing of investment projects under Plan for Coal.

Report on comparability study between German and English coal mines

by
Mr J Marshall and Professor C T Shaw

1. **INTRODUCTION**

   We were originally requested by the MMC to consider the possibility of comparing the technical efficiency of the UK coal mining industry with that of other coal mining countries. After a preliminary study, it was concluded that a valid comparison between countries and even between whole mines in different countries could not properly be made, because of irreconcilable differences in the size of mines, layouts, working practices and facilities and geological factors.

   It was, however, felt that a reasonable comparison might be made between individual coal faces in different countries provided that broadly similar mining conditions could be found.

   A consideration of a number of cases led us to the conclusion that such a comparison would best be done at mines in West Germany and this report sets out the results of the exercise done between there and the UK.

2. **CONCLUSIONS**

   1. The productive efficiency on coal faces in British mines which have been modernised is not significantly different from that on comparable coal faces at similarly modern mines in West Germany.

      In view of the extensive co-operation between the industries of the two countries which was noted during the visits, this is perhaps not surprising.

   2. OMS based on saleable tonnes is used in both countries and is a reasonably good general measure of productivity in terms of product sold but it is not on its own a satisfactory basis for comparison of performance between faces in either country, let alone between countries.

      Alternative tests have been applied based on gross tonnage won, volume of mineral won and the area of the seam extracted. The results have not led us to the conclusion that any face was significantly more efficient than the others.

   3. All the mines visited, both in Britain and in Germany, would benefit by increasing the proportion of the shift spent on the coal face and the proportion of the latter time in which coal was actually being won. The management in both countries are fully conscious of this and are actively working to achieve better results.

   4. The face equipment currently in use is capable of higher production. To achieve this there is a need for the reliabiltity of both face equipment and

other equipment in the mining system to be improved to reduce delays. There is a need to ensure that all equipment between the face and the surface is fully capable of handling the maximum output produceable by the face equipment.

5. Any apparent difference in productivity between the two countries on a national basis does not seem to arise from differences in mining skills. It is more likely to arise from the fact that the German management have been able to close down uneconomic and inefficient pits more readily than has been achieved in the UK.

6. To a great extent the two countries tend to purchase only equipment manufactured from within their home country. We believe that some benefit would accrue by greater interchange in this area. A welcome indication of this trend was noted at Creswell where the power loader was of Eickhoff manufacture to a British design.

3. THE PROBLEMS OF SELECTION OF COMPARABLE FACES

Originally it was hoped to find matching faces in a range of different thicknesses—thin, medium and thick. It was also essential that the selection should be from faces on which coal was won by shearers because it is from such machines that almost all British longwall output is obtained (there are only a handful of UK faces on which ploughs are used) and comparison between the two different systems of coal winning would not produce valid results. In the event it was found that there were no coal faces at all in the Ruhr using shearers in a thickness of less than 1·7 metres.

The principal reason for this difference of working lies in differing geological features. The strength of most coal seams in Germany is significantly less than most seams in the UK and this feature combined with certain structural factors in the seams makes the coal more readily "ploughable" in Germany. Ploughing is favoured in thin seams where possible because of the reduced size and complexity of the coal winning equipment—an important matter in restricted space. An additional factor favouring ploughs is that, in general, the strength and hardness of the floor strata is greater than in the UK.

In addition, in the light of the fact that the German Industry has had the opportunity to modernise completely, we had to confine our search for matching UK faces to those pits in the UK which have the most modern equipment. As a result the faces chosen were from mines which are making an operating profit.

Thus of the three working faces studied in Germany, one was of medium working height and the other two were thick.

The three faces studied in the UK were respectively thin, medium and thick.

4. BRIEF DESCRIPTION OF FACES CHOSEN

4.1 Kellingley   Beeston Seam   79s Face

A single unit face 230 metres long retreating slightly to the rise in a seam 2·87 metres thick (including dirt bands) of which 2·28 metres is extracted plus 16cms of soft floor strata. The depth is about 720 metres. The coal is moderately hard, the floor a soft fireclay and the roof a weak shale which is contained by leaving some roof coal. Coal is won on the major length of face by a 150 Kw double ended ranging drum shearer and for 25 metres near the tail gate by a 150 Kw single ended ranging drum shearer, the coal being conveyed on heavy duty armoured face conveyor and stage loaders. The face is supported by Dowty 4/300 chock shield powered supports with appropriate matching buttress, packhole and roadhead supports at the face ends.

4.2 Ollerton   Parkgate Seam   33s Face

A single unit face 259 metres long advancing slightly to the dip in a seam 181 cm thick of which 180 cm is extracted plus 11 cm of soft floor dirt. The depth is about 750 metres. The coal is moderately hard, the floor a soft fireclay, and the roof a moderately hard mudstone. Coal is won by a 150 Kw double-ended ranging drum shearer cutting the full length of the face and coal being conveyed on heavy duty armoured face conveyor and stage loader. Roads were made by advance headings driven by side discharge Dosco heading machines. The face is supported by Dowty 4/300 chock shield powered supports with appropriate buttress and packhole supports.

4.3 Niederberg   Girondelle 5 Seam   Panel 126

A single unit face 200 metres long retreating slightly to the dip in a seam 1·70 metres thick, including 11 cm of dirt all of which is extracted. The depth was about 580 metres. The coal was a moderately hard non-coking type with a shale roof and sandy shale floor. Coal was got by an Eickhoff EDW 340 Kw double ended ranging drum shearer loading on to a heavy duty armoured conveyor. The main length of the face was supported by Hemscheidt KG 280 caliper shield supports operating on the "one web back" principle. One roadway was second use from the previous panel and the other newly driven for this panel.

4.4 Ewald   Q/W Seam   4a Face

A single unit face 260 metres long advancing on the strike in a seam with a dip of about 9 degrees. The seam was 239 cm thick including 34 cm of dirt bands all of which was won by an Eickhoff EDW–2L–2W double-ended 150 Kw ranging drum shearer loading on to a heavy duty armoured face conveyor. The main length of face is supported by Westfalia chock shield powered supports type BS 2.1. One roadway is second use from the previous panel and the other driven as an advance heading.

4.5 Creswell   Threequarter Seam   32s Face

A single unit face 268 metres long advancing slightly to the rise in a seam 84 cm thick all of which is extracted plus 6 cm of soft floor strata. The depth is about 720 metres. The coal is fairly hard, the floor a soft siltstone and the roof a moderate silty mudstone. Coal is won by a floor based Eickhoff double ended 175 Kw ranging drum shearer of German manufacture to a British design. The main gate was driven as an advanced heading and the tail gate ripped behind the face. The face is supported by Dowty thin seam powered supports with appropriate matching packhole supports.

100

4.6 **Walsum   E/F Seam   52s Face**

A single unit face 272 metres long in a seam 1·87 metres thick of which 24 cm consisted of dirt bands. The face was a retreat panel between two worked out panels and the re-use of roadways at both ends was practised. The depth was about 650 metres. The coal was moderately soft and the roof and floor of moderate shale. On the main length of face coal was won by an Eickhoff EDW 230–2 double ended 230 Kw ranging drum shearer and on the remainder by a similar Eickhoff 170–1 170 Kw shearer loading on to a heavy duty armoured face conveyor. The main length of face was supported by Hemscheid KG 280 caliper shield powered supports.

5. COMPARISONS OF FACES VISITED

A series of tables—Tables 1 to 6—has been prepared from the data obtained from the mines. It is important that Annex 2 be read in conjunction with any study of the tables.

5.1 **The life of working panels**

The life of any face—the distance it is planned to advance or retreat—is controlled by a number of factors some of them outside the control of the management, but sometimes a matter of choice. Long life, where practicable, is advantageous because it minimises non-productive work such as opening out new faces and then transfer of equipment from face to face.

In Germany there are some statutory controls on the distance of advance permitted but there are provisions for extending this where conditions are suitable.

In the UK there are no statutory restrictions of a direct nature, but in any case the conditions of ventilation, roadway maintenance, respirable dust, etc, must be maintained in compliance with general statute to allow a face to continue to work. The further a face travels the more difficult it becomes to maintain satisfactory conditions in respect of these factors.

The faces chosen for study in the UK had an advantage of longer life as compared with those seen in Germany. This can be seen by studying the figures for panel life shown in Table 1.B.

5.2 **Ventilation and firedamp**

5.2.1 *General*

The maintenance of satisfactory ventilation conditions is important in enabling management to keep production flowing and we observed some differences in this respect, as follows:—

(*a*) WEST GERMANY

Two of the faces operated with limited systems of firedamp drainage but one managed without this. The firedamp given off varied from 0·4 cu. metres/tonne to 7·6 cu. m./tonne.

In no circumstances did it seem likely that firedamp would limit the working of the faces visited.

101

TABLE 1A

GEOLOGICAL	FACE	CRESWELL (UK) 32s	NIEDERBERG (G) 126	WALSUM (G) E/F 52	OLLERTON (UK) 33s	EWALD (G) Q W4a	KELLINGLEY (UK) 79s
1. Depth	M	720	580	650	750	840 to 910	725 to 710
2. Coal thickness	M	·86(·84)*	1·59	1·64 (1·76)*	1·73 (1·75)*	1·57 (1·77)(2·05)*	2·13
3. Thickness coal plus dirt bands	M	·86 (·84)	1·70	1·87 (1·93)	(1·81)	2·27 (2·66)(2·39)	2·87 (3·00)
4. Cut thickness	M	·94 (·90)	1·70	1·87 (1·93)	1·95 (1·91)	2·27 (2·66)(2·39)	Total Coal Dirt 2·44 1·77 67
5. Dip	o	1:25 rising	10°	5°	1-20 dipping	9°	"gentle"
6. Gas content	M³/T	28·72	7·6	Not given – gas observed to be minimal	5·78	0·4	16
7. Other seams mined		Top hard 280M above, Hazel 410M above, Clowne 525M above	NIL	NIL	One – Top hard 200 M above	NIL	NIL
8. Coal type Volatiles %		35%	12·5%	32·5%	34%		38% (Medium hard cleated)
9. Roof measures		Silty mudstone	Shale	Shale	Mudstone	Sandstone	Weak shales or mudstones
10. Floor measures		Siltstone	Sandy shale	Shale	Seatearth	Soft fireclay or silty mudstone	

*Figures in brackets indicate other thicknesses given but not used for making comparisons.

PHYSICAL	FACE		CRESWELL (UK) 32s	NIEDERBERG (G) 126	WALSUM (G) E/F 52	OLLERTON (UK) 33s	EWALD (G) Q W4a	KELLINGLEY (UK) 79s
11. Density coal		T/M³	1·3998	1·361	1·300	1·320	1·545	1·34
12. Density dirt		T/M³	2·4674	2·5*	2·5*	2·510	3·072	1·86 (1·71 to 2·0)
13. Density material cut		T/M³	1·495	1·434	1·448	1·454	2·016	1·482
14. Panel life		M	800	650	1020	2300	400	1050
15. Face length		M	268	200	272 (270)**	259 (252)**	261 (260)**	230
16. Method			Advance	Retreat	Retreat	Advance	Advance	Retreat
17. Water			Some—not serious	NIL	Not a problem	Present—pumping required		Not a problem
18. Geological problems			Adverse—conditions—broken roof etc.	None				Minor—small faults
19. Dust			3·7 mgms/M³ in return	Observed to be dusty on visit—but not production stop		3.3 mgms/M³		
20. Effective temp	°C					Aircooling installed 27·2°	Shorter shift required +28° air cooling	25°
21. Distance from shaft M			3450	5700	3800	2800	4800	4100

*Assumed figure.

**Other face lengths given but not used.

Note: Where gaps in the information are shown, those figures were not obtained from the mines.

TABLE 2

		CRESWELL (UK)	NIEDERBERG (G)	WALSUM (G)	OLLERTON (UK)	EWALD (G)	KELLINGLEY (UK)
SHIFT TIMES (5)							
1. Official shift (4) length	Min	435	480	480	435	420	435
2. Travelling time	Min	75	113 (130)	16 (120)	79	104	84
3. Preparation and meal times	Min	30	30	30	30	30	30
4. Time on face	Min	330	337 (320)	334 (330)	326	286	321
DELAYS							
English mines							
5. Total	Min/Shift	146·3			105·0		57·4
German mines							
6. Long delays	Min/Shift			84·5		60	
7. Short delays	Min/Shift			34·1		102	
8. Total	Min/Shift		175·8	118·6		162	
9. Standard machine(1) time	Min/Shift	161	161·2	215·4	160	124	134
10. Machine available(2) to cut	Min/Shift	183·7		249·5	221	226	263·4
11. Machine cutting(3) time	Min/Shift	111	144	188	150	126	156

(1) Time on face less delays for German mines—Figure given as standard for English mines.

(2) Time on face less long delays for German mines—Time on face less delays for English mines.

(3) Arrived at by dividing tonnage produced per shift by cutting rate expressed in tonnes/minute.

(4) English shift times are shaft bottom to shaft bottom.

(5) The German shift times are bank to bank—including hoisting time therefore.

TABLE 3

STAFF	CRESWELL	NIEDERBERG	WALSUM	OLLERTON	EWALD	KELLINGLEY
COAL FACE—PRODUCTION						
1. Shearer Operators	2 2 – 4	2 2 – 4	3 3 2 – 8	2 – 2 – 4	3 3 3 3 12	2 2 – 4
2. 2nd Shearer Operators			2 2 1 1 6			2 2 – 4
3. AFC Rammers	3 3 – 6	2 2 2 6	1 1 1 – 3	2 – 2 – 4	1 1 1 1 4	1 1 – 2
4. Shield Operators	6 6 – 12	9 7 4 20	6 6 4 2 18	5 – 5 – 10	2 1 1 1 5	3+1 3+1 – 8
5. Maingate End	5 5 – 10	4 2 – 6	2 2 4 – 8	5 – 5 – 10	4 4 4 4 16	4 4 – 8
6. Tailgate End			1 2 2 – 5		3 3 3 3 12	4 4 – 8
7. Chargeman		1 1 – 2	1 1 3 – 5		1 – – – 1	1 1 – 2
8. TOTAL	16 16 – 32	18 14 6 38	16 16 15 6 53	14 – 14 – 28	14 12 12 12 50	18 18 – 36
OTHER WORK FACE						
9. Cross Slit Men	1 1 – 2					2 2 – 4
10. Methane Drainage				1·25		NOT GIVEN
11. Roof Bolting		– – 2 2				2 – – 2
12. Resin Men		– 1 1 2	1 1 1 1 4		3 3 – – 6	
13. Air Machine Operator		– 1 1 2				
14. Transfer Face to Gate		– – 2 2			1 1 1 1 4	
15. Face Maintenance	– – 2 2			– 4 – 4		
16. Production Control Cent						
17. Development		1 1 – 2			6 5 6 5 22	
18. TOTAL	1 1 2 4	1 3 6 10	1 1 1 1 4	1·25 – 4 4 5·25	10 9 7 6 32	4 2 – 6
19. TOTAL ON FACE	17 17 2 36	19 17 12 48	17 17 16 7 57	15·25 14 18 7 33·25	24 21 19 18 82	22 20 – 42
ENGINEERING						
20. Fitters	2 2 2 6	2 0 16 18	2 2 2 4 10	2 2 2 6	5 4 4 6 19	2 2 1 5
21. Electricians	2 2 1 5	2 2 2 6		1 1 1 3		2 2 1 5
22. Chock Fitters	1 1 – 2	1 1 2 4		1 1 – 2		1 1 – 2
23. Charge Fitters	1 – – 1	1 1 1 3		1 – – 1		1 1 – 2
Unclassified					1 – – – 1	
24. TOTAL ENGINEERING	6 5 3 14	6 4 21 31	2 2 2 4 10	5 4 3 12	6 4 4 6 20	6 6 2 14
25. TOTAL ON FACE	23 22 5 50	25 21 33 79	19 19 18 11 67	20·25 18 7 45·25	30 25 23 24 102	28 26 2 56

105

TABLE 4

PRODUCTION STATISTICS

	CRESWELL (UK)	NIEDERBERG (G)	WALSUM (G)	OLLERTON (UK)	EWALD (G)	KELLINGLEY (UK)
1. Period	Year to June 82	5 months Feb-June 82	9 months to June 82	March to June 82	9 days in July 82	Year to June 82
2. Machine shifts per day	2·33	2·04	2·79	2·38	3·78	2·56
3. Maintenance shifts	1	1	1	1	1	1
4. Strips per shift	1·97	4·2 (est)	2·15	2·07	2·59	2·48
5. Advances per day M	2·662 (3·119)*	4·94	3·61	2·717	4·98	3·625
6. Advances per shift M	1·143 (1·263)*	2·42	1·29	1·138m	1·32	1·414
7. Depth of cut—web M	0·58		·60 (0·625)	0·55	·51	0·57
8. Cutting rate M²/Min	2·76	3·37	1·87	1·969	2·76	2·086
9. Tonnes per shift T	430 (438)**	1180 (1047)**	950 (754)**	836 (750)	1574 (835)**	1011 (920)**
10. Tonnes per day T	1003 (1022)**	2408 (2136)**	2651 (2105)**	1990 (1787)	5948 (3155)**	2592 (2357)**
11. Number of Shearers	1	1	2	1	1	2

*July–December 1981.

**Saleable tonnes.

TABLE 5

FACE EQUIPMENT	CRESWELL (UK)	NIEDERBERG (G)	WALSUM (G)	OLLERTON (UK)	EWALD (G)	KELLINGLEY (UK)
1. Shearer 1	Eickhoff floor based DE Buttock 175 KW 0·91m × 0·76m	Eickhoff Derds EDW 340 KW 1·4 × 0·675m	EDW 230–2 Derds 230 KW 1·6m × 0·625m	A/S Derds 150 KW 1·68m × 0·61m	EDW Derds 26 2W 150 KW 1·6m × 0·85m	A/S Derds 150 KW 1·83m × 0·762m
2. Shearer 2			EDW 170–1 Derds 170 KW 1·6m × ·625m			A/S Derds 150 KW 1·83m × ·762m
3. A.F.C.	Twin outboard chain. 190mm wide, 19mm chain	Double middle chain 30 × 108mm chain	Double middle chain EKF 3 732mm × 1500mm —26mm chain	Twin outboard chain 222mm wide 22mm chain	D.M.K. EKF 3 300mm wide 26mm chain	NCB Spec H.D. AFC Twin outboard 222mm wide 22mm chain
4. A.F.C. Head Drive	Mining supplies 112 KW North Notts	2 × 120 KW	2 × 160 KW	Mining supplies/North Notts 112 KW	2 × 200 KW	Huwood P300 1 × 224 KW
5. Tail Drive	Winster/North Notts 112 KW Low seam	2 × 120 KW	2 × 160 KW Klockner Becorit Coal Breaker	Mining supplies/North Notts 112 KW	1 × 200 KW DLB 1000 Breaker	M.S. 1 × 186 KW
6. Supports Main	Dowty thin seam powered supports	Hemscheidt KG 280	Hemscheidt KG 280	Dowty 4/300 chock shields	Westfalia chock shield BS 2–1	146 Dowty 4/400 C.S. 102/53' 1·5m
7. Tail Gate end	Arches Dowty 4/160 Packhole	TH Arches Bars and Hydraulic props	Re-used old road TH Arches Slide bars, hydraulic or wood props	Advance heading—Arches Gullick 6/240 Packhole Supports	Re-used old road Props and bars	1 × 6/450 Buttress, 1 × 4/300 Buttress, 1 × 4/450 packhole 1 N/Yorks Roadhead
8. Head Gate end	Advance heading arches Dowty 4/160 Packhole Supports	TH Arches. A double row of wooden props anhydrite pack	Re-used old road TH Arches Slide bars, hydraulic or wood props	Advance heading—Arches Gullick 6/240 Packhole Supports	Advanced heading TH arches Props and bars	as above for Tail
9. Stage loader	0·664m 48 KW 500 TPH	92cm	2 × 120 KW	30' = 0·762m 90 KW 600 TPH	0·800mm EKF 111 63 KW	0·600m NCB fixed beam 90 KW

107

Table 6 Comparisons

		CRESWELL (UK)	NIEDERBERG (G)	WALSUM (G)	OLLERTON (UK)	EWALD (G)	KELLINGLEY (UK)
Official Shift length	Min	435	480	480	435	420	435
Time on face	Min	330	337	334	326	286	321
Machine Available To Cut (MATC)	Min	184	(Estimate) (219)	250	221	226	263
Machine Cutting Time	Min	111	144	188	150	126	156
% of TOF Cutting	%	34	43	56	45	44	49
% of MATC Cutting	%	60	66	75	68	56	59
Potential Production per shift	T	1280	2769	1691	1820	3613	2421
	M²	910·8¹	1135·7	624·6	641·9	789·4	669·6
Actual Production per shift	T	430	1180	950	836	1574	1011
	M²	306·3	484·0	350·9	294·9	344·5	325·2
Volume cut per day	M³	671	1680	1836	1372	2951	2034
Area cut per day	M²	713	988	982	704	1300	834
OMS—Face men only —saleable	T	27·6	56·2	39·7	66·4	64·4	51·2
OMS—Face men only —Total	T	27·0	63·4	50·0	60·3	121·4	56·3
OMS—Face men only	M²	19·3	26	18·5	21·3	26·5	18·1
OMS—Face men only	M³	18·1	44·2	34·6	41·6	60·2	44·2
OMS—All workers at face excl. engineering total	T	24·4	50·2	46·5	52·0	73·5	49·8
OMS—All workers at face—total	T	18·2	30·5	39·6	39·6	58·9	39·3

¹Note that it was reported to us that Creswell on the 32s face actually achieved 960M² in one working shift.

(b) UNITED KINGDOM

In all three UK faces intensive firedamp drainage systems were needed, in one case with both upward and downward cross measure boreholes, to maintain satisfactory conditions. Even then there were occasions when the firedamp content approached statutory levels at which point all work must cease. Firedamp given off varied from 5·78 cu. metres/tonne to 16·0 cu. m/tonne.

Although there was no evidence that output had actually been restricted by ventilation requirements on the faces studied, those in the UK were much more liable to that situation than the German faces. As would be expected more labour was employed on firedamp drainage work in the UK.

5.2.2 *Respirable dust*

There are times when high levels of respirable dust can restrict production activity on a coal face and we examined the different control procedures in each country.

In the UK the law sets certain limits for the faces and if these are not met the face is subject to 'sanctions' in which remedial action has to be taken which may reduce production. If the first measures are not successful further sanctions may apply which can completely halt production.

In Germany we were told that the restrictive limits do not apply to the face but that the monitoring applies to each workman and records keep a measure of the total 'dust loading' to which he has been subjected. When certain levels are reached the workman concerned is taken off face work for a period of time and put to work in relatively dust free places until his average dust loading has diminished enough to allow his return to the face.

Although it was not possible for us to make precise comparisons because of different bases for measurement, our observations led us to the view that certain visible respirable dust conditions seen in Germany would have been likely to be subject to sanctions under the UK systems of control.

5.3 Support

5.3.1 *On the face line*

On all six coal faces self-advancing powered supports were used. In each case the supports were of 'home' manufacture, but this is usual in both countries—there has been very little interchange of each other's supports. In Germany two of the faces used Caliper Shield Supports which normally have just two main hydraulic elements operating in inclined attitude and with the travelling track on the face side of the unit. One German face and two UK faces used Chock Shield Supports with four near vertical hydraulic elements and the travelling track between the two lines of vertical supports. In the other UK case a chock type of special design for thin seams was used.

Generally we found little significant difference between the performance of comparable powered supports in each country. Equally, where heavy duty shield and chock shield types were in use their period of service below ground sometimes, with direct transfer from finished to newly opened faces, appeared comparable with broadly similar maintenance requirements.

5.3.2 *At roadheads and face ends*

From the faces visited we noted that those in the UK more often used powered supports specially designed for this area—buttress supports for the waste edge, packhole supports near the gate side and in some cases special designs in the roadhead itself. In the German faces the usual supports in this area were types of link bar or girder in conjunction with hand-set hydraulic props. In this respect we considered the UK systems to be superior.

5.4 Retreat and advance working

Of the faces studied in the UK one was working retreat (Kellingley) and two advance (Ollerton and Creswell). Of those in Germany two were retreating (Walsum and Niederberg) and one advancing (Ewald).

A noticeable difference between the retreat faces was that at Kellingley it had proved necessary to drive both roads in the solid to the extremity of the panel and protection pillars of about 90 metres width were left between panels. Even then, forward abutment pressures from the face were significant, particularly at the return gate where a "slit gate" arrangement was necessary to give proper control of the strata and a ventilation system to prevent the risk of accessible firedamp at the return end of the face.

In Walsum both roads had been formed during the working of previous panels and were being used for a second time. Strata movement in both roof and floor was evident but not sufficient to cause serious problems. In Niederberg one roadway had been formed on a previous panel and was being used for a second time without difficulty; the other road had been driven for the panel being worked.

These facts indicated that the natural geological conditions were more favourable to retreat working on the two German faces than they were on the face in the UK.

5.5 Comparisons of the figures obtained from the mines

Comments have been made in the notes to the tables, and in other sections of this report on the difficulty of making comparisons. Table 6 is a direct attempt to make various comparisons of the efficiency of the various faces.

The initial problem was to define efficiency. The normal figure used on both sides of the channel is OMS—saleable tonnes of coal output per man-shift. The problem with this figure is that a saleable tonne can vary from clean coal, from which as much as 50% of the material mined has been washed, to a relatively dirty coal containing as much as 20% ash content—some of which may actually have been added after mining.

When to this is added the difficulty of analysing just which man-shifts are included by the mines when calculating OMS, it becomes clear that OMS as currently produced is not comparable between mines.

We have therefore investigated other measures of efficiency. These are:—

(a) Times—how much of the available shift time is actually spent on the face and how much of the time on the face is spent actually producing coal.

(b) Potential production compared with actual production. Given that the shearer in each individual case can cut only at a rate conditions allow, then it is possible to estimate how much can be cut with no delays and compare this with how much is actually cut on average. This gives a measure of the efficiency of utilisation. This calculation is done on an area basis and on a tonnage basis to indicate the effect of density of mined material.

(c) Output per man-shift. An attempt was made to obtain manning figures that were comparable. OMS has been calculated, using these figures on total mineral tons mined per man-shift, volume of mineral cut per man-shift and area of the seam mined per man-shift basis.

(a) WORKING TIMES

The actual official length of the shift in England is shorter than that of two of the German mines (Table 2). The shift length in England is officially 7·25 hours shaft bottom to shaft bottom plus one hoisting time, (which is normally assumed to be 30 minutes) while times in Germany are bank to bank. However, the critical time is the Time On the Face which is not significantly different between countries as the English faces visited averaged shorter travelling times. (Note that the NCB also refers to this time as Machine Available Time (MAT) which must not be confused with what we have called Machine Available to Cut Time (MACT).

The time the shearers were actually cutting is a calculated figure derived as shown in Annex 3. These calculations involve the use of the 'instantaneous cutting rate' figures discussed under Table 4, Annex 2. Other than these calculated cutting rates the rest of the information was given by the mines. It is felt that these figures are therefore comparable.

There does not seem to be a significant difference in the percentage of TOF used for cutting between the German and English pits, with the exception of Creswell. Creswell, it must be stressed, was also the pit with the thinnest seam (just over half the thickness of the next thinnest seen seam) and maintenance and the correction of breakdowns inevitably will take longer in heights of less than 1 metre. In addition this face was nearing the end of its life and efficiencies have fallen off in recent months—it was doing better previously.

When percentage of Machine Available to Cut Time (MACT) (the Face Available Time less the long delays recorded) is used, the picture changes. This illustrates the fact that the thinner seams—which have

111

relatively greater time lost by long rather than short delays—gain more than the thicker seams in efficiency.

However, the figures for the percentage of time on the face actually used for cutting show that all the mines, both English and German have room for improvement if breakdowns and delays can be reduced.

(*b*) Potential compared with actual production

These figures illustrate in tonnes and square metres, the difference that would have been made had there been no delays on the faces visited.

(*c*) OMS Figures

The labour figures shown in Table 3 are all based on 2 or 3 or even 4 shift working. However, in Table 4 it will be noted that the average production shifts worked per day are figures like 2·56 or 3·78. This arises from the practice of all mines visited of maintaining spare capacity in the form of available spare shifts. However, there are some tasks in any face which tend to be performed only on one shift. If these are tasks which do not interfere with production they will almost always be performed on normal day shift. If, however, they might interfere with production, they tend to be performed on the off shift. Methane drainage for example falls in the latter category.

This problem has resulted in the production shifts not each having the same number of personnel, even on the same mine. To calculate the OMS therefore either a range of figures—depending on the numbers actually shown on shift—has to be produced, or some other system must be adopted.

As it happens, the 3 German mines have all shown full production staff for, say, 3 shifts where they have averaged 2·79 shifts actually, while the 3 English pits have shown staff for two shifts where they have averaged 2·33. (Note that Kellingley did give us figures for 2 and 3 shift working although the table only shows the 2 shift figures.)

In the OMS calculated therefore—for the face production men only—the English figures of men on face were increased by the amount of the additional shift fraction. Then, to allow for the shift differentials mentioned above the daily output tonnage has been divided by the daily labour force to give the OMS figure shown.

A study of the various OMS figures produced shows that the 'merit table' changed depending on which measure one chooses to use. Note that Ewald with its four daily production shifts and high densities generally comes out first. However, every other mine with the exception of Creswell comes second at least once. Creswell with its very thin seam is technically less comparable. As far as the comparability exercise is concerned therefore, the only conclusion reachable is that there is no significant difference between the countries which can be highlighted from this work.

5.6 **Other features**

At one of the German mines visited, environmental conditions were responsible for some limitation of production because of high underground temperature and humidity—this was effected by reducing the shift time from eight to seven hours (See note on Tables, Annex 2).

The control of deposited coal dust in roadways is different in the two countries. In the UK it is done by the application of limestone dust to maintain a prescribed incombustible content. In Germany it is more often done by the application of hygroscopic chemicals to 'bind' the dust so that it cannot be raised into an explosive cloud. The German system seems to have the disadvantage of causing much corrosion of roadway supports where there is prolonged exposure. This factor appears to be of no significance in a comparison of efficiencies.

Much other information was given to us (Annex 1). For example, some details of maintenance programmes were given, as was more information on delays. Some mines gave the information on the original installation of the face equipment. This information has proved invaluable for background but no valid comparisons could be drawn from what was available without significant further studies on the mines. In the light of the conclusions on comparative productivity reached in this report, it was not considered that further effort would materially alter the result.

6. INTERNATIONAL CO-OPERATION

During the visit to Germany we saw a good deal of evidence of regular and detailed exchange of technical information between UK and German engineers and research and development workers. Such exchanges have apparently been carried out in a wide ranging and established formal fashion for at least eight years and informally for some time before that. The exchange appears to be full and frank, and much mutual benefit is obtained. This may be one reason why standards between the countries are not significantly different.

7. ACKNOWLEDGEMENTS

We would like to acknowledge our gratitude to many people who helped so much towards our carrying out this exercise. The managers and their support staff at all the six mines visited were most courteous and helpful, giving very readily all the information we requested. The Area Director and other higher managerial officials ensured that the arrangements gave us the opportunity to carry out the exercise as we wished.

In particular, we thank Herr Baethmann of RAG, Essen and Mr T L Carr of MRDE, Bretby for all the work they did in setting up the detailed arrangements and ensuring that everything worked smoothly.

113

Figures required for each face

The principle is that we require the 'basic' figures so that we can do our own calculations as to the efficiencies etc. We do not really require derived figures such as OMS—but will obviously look at them too.

Information required

1. *Geological and physical*

   Depth
   Geological section showing
      Coal seams—thickness, quality, hardness;
      Roof and floor strata—quality, geomechanical measures;
      Dip.
   Information gas content, water;
   Other seams—are they being or have they been mined?;
   Distance from main outlet;
   Geological disturbances (faults, rolls, channels);
   Face length and dimensions; and
   % Extraction.

2. *Face equipment*

   Type, make, duty, numbers of face equipment;
   Original cost; and
   Original capital estimate used to justify mining.

3. *Support equipment*

   Gate equipment back to where coal from this face joins other coal.

4. *Maintenance*

   Details of planned maintenance programme;
   Maintenance staffing;
   Details of all breakdowns during previous period;
   Time coal actually being cut;
   Time all machines operational but coal not being cut; and
   Delays—listing with causes.

5. *Staffing*

   Listing of all staff employed on the face at any time;
   Time spent on face. Actual job;
   Travelling time;
   Rest and meal periods allowed;
   Overlap, shift times, shift lengths;
   Installation of original equipment—staff employed;
   Time taken;
   Staff not on face but handling coal to junction point; and
   Working days.

6. *Production*

   Historical production figures—coal tonnes produced;
   Instantaneous cutting rate;
   Details of how this is measured; and
   Correlation between planned and achieved.

Notes on the preparation of the tables

Introduction

From the information gathered from the mines a number of comparison tables have been prepared. In the first instance each mine was sent (Annex 1) a questionnaire which indicated the information required. Each mine in fact did an excellent job of preparing a dossier on the face to be visited, which contained the bulk of the information required.

Inevitably, due to differences of interpretation of what was required and also due to differences in the statistics actually kept by the mines, much work needed to be done, firstly to assess what information was already in the files and to try to understand the basis on which the information was compiled. Then an attempt to compare the basic figures could be made.

In some cases, the figures had to be calculated from those given in the dossiers and in others, more than one figure is given by the mine for the same item. For these and other various reasons these notes need to be read with the tables as they show how the results were obtained.

TABLE 1a   GEOLOGICAL DATA

The mines have been tabled in order of increasing thickness of seam mined. Originally the mines were to be split into pairs which were intended to be compared specifically with each other. These pairs were to have been Creswell and Niederberg, Walsum and Ollerton and Ewald and Kellingley. In the event the table has been prepared so that each face can be compared with every other face. The number of the face visited is listed below the name of the mine.

1. Depth

In most cases the depth was given. As in almost all cases as there was some dip, one depth does not give the whole picture. However, for comparative purposes, the depths are not critical, and the depths given are adequate. Note than in the case of Creswell the depth given is clearly stated as the average for the four working faces currently active on the mine—which, given the flat dip is not a problem. Ollerton gives a depth for the 'Parkgate workings' which again appears to be an average for the seam as a whole. However, all faces visited were relatively deep, the shallowest being Niederberg at 580m and the deepest, Ewald, at over 840m. All faces had some strata problems, but as far as this comparison is concerned, it can be said that the faces were as comparable in this respect as is practicable to find.

2. Thicknesses—items 2 to 4 on Table 1a

The presentation of the thicknesses differed, the Germans generally giving coal and dirt separately. In general, the German seams are mined to the seam boundaries and any coal left on the roof or floor is not worth getting. Any dirt mined was internal to the seam. In England there is often some coal left on the roof for stability and there is generally some dirt cut from the floor, again for reasons of better floor conditions. In addition, in the dossiers there is often conflicting information given. Ewald, for example, gives a section which shows 2·05m coal and 0·34m of dirt, with a full cut of 2·39m. However, in the table showing production from all faces, the face visited, Q W4a, shows 1·57m coal and 0·70m dirt for a cut of 2·27m. Again, in Anlage 1·1, the coal is given as 1·77m, dirt as 0·89m for a total of 2·66m. The production figures seem to be the ones most relateable to the actual tonnages mined and were therefore accepted. In the case of the English seams, in each case a section is given showing the coal, dirt and actual location of the cut. In the case of Ollerton, the thickness of the included waste is not shown and so has been measured off to scale. It must be noted though that we did obtain actual data for the 33s face for the last 4 weeks before our visit. Here the thicknesses were 1·73 coal with a cut of 1·95m and these actuals have been accepted. For Creswell the section shows 84cm of coal and a dirt cut of 6cm. However, again, actual production figures show 86cm of coal and 8cm of dirt. In each case we have accepted what seemed the most recent figures as those to use.

3. **Dip—Item 5 Table 1a**

In no case was the dip significant though it must be stated that at one end of the face at Ewald, where the advance heading was, it was steepening sharply. However, none of the dips was such as to affect the mining efficiency of the longwalls.

4. **Gas—Item 6 Table 1a**

The gas was given in terms of cubic metres of gas given off per tonne of saleable coal produced, except for Walsum which did not give figures as their gas content was so low as to be no problem. It must be noted that all 3 English pits have significant gas and all were resorting to methane drainage, while only two of the German pits—Niederberg and Ewald had enough gas to require methane drainage. This is a significant difference as it gives a possible source of production loss in the English pits which does not exist in their German counterparts. This is discussed further in the ventilation section of the report.

5. **Other seams mined**

Two of the English pits, Creswell and Ollerton, were mining seams in areas where other seams had previously been mined out. The other 4 mines had mined other seams, but not in the area where the faces visited were working. It must be noted that this is not considered to have had any relevance to the relative efficiencies in the faces visited.

6. **Coal type—Roof measures and floor measures**

These are listed as shown in the reports. In general, English coal is relatively hard and the roof and floor rocks weak, while German coal is soft between hard roof and floor. This has led to the more extensive use of ploughs on German faces and also to the fact that the German mines can almost always extract the coal to roof and do not need to cut extra dirt down to a good floor. In addition, fewer pillars are needed in the German pits leading to generally higher extraction percentages.

TABLE 1b PHYSICAL DATA

7. Densities

These were not initially given but calculations soon showed that there were major differences in density and they would be required. The range is from $1 \cdot 421$ t/m³ to $2 \cdot 016$ t/m³. Clearly, the tonnage that must be moved per unit volume cut varies with density. Further confusion is added to the picture by the fact that all the tonnes reported are 'tonnes saleable'. These may or may not contain added ash. The mines have since been asked for densities, but actual figures were only available for 3 when work started on this report.

8. Panel life

This was the original life of the longwall, not the life remaining when the face was visited. There is a major difference between English and German practice in this area, discussed elsewhere. In general, the faces in English pits tend to have a longer life.

9. Face length

All the reports give a face length—which appears generally to be a rounded figure. This comment arises from the fact that in 4 cases actual face lengths were given in other data and these varied by unit metres from the standard lengths given, but not to a significant extent. In all cases where more accurate data is available, what appears to be the more correct figure has been accepted.

TABLE 2

1. The official shift time is taken from the data given—note that only in the case of Ewald, where it is one hour less than the other German mines due to the high effective mean temperature is there any significant difference. The time on the face works out much the same for all mines, again with the exception of Ewald. Travelling time is, of course, dependent on the distance of the face from the shaft. Since the British faces were in general closer to the shaft, the shorter travelling times make up for the shorter official shift period.

2. Delays.

There is no correlation in the recording of delays. The British and German practices differ and as a result the delays have been shown separately. It must be noted too that the delays shown were, in the case of all three British pits, the averages for the June quarter. This means that they do not correlate exactly with the production period for which figures are available. The Germans split their delays into long delays—in four categories—and short delays—less than 10 minutes and these too do not always correlate with the production period studied. Since the data were so different only totals have been shown as the other, more detailed figures are not able to be compared.

It is the opinion of the consultants that the German long delays are probably the equivalent of the delays recorded in the British pits and that the short delays in Germany may not all be actually recorded but may partly be estimates such that 'Laufzeit' is the actual machine cutting time. In other words, we suspect that the British do not record the equivalent delays given as short delays by the Germans.

118

If this assumption is correct, comparing German long delays with British delays there is no significant difference. However, if the short delays are included in the German figures, the British would appear more efficient.

3. **Items 9, 10, and 11.**

Standard Machine Running Time is a figure given as a result of Work Study by Creswell and Ollerton. It is assumed to correlate with Laufzeit or machine running time as calculated as a real average achievement by the German pits. Machine Available to Cut Time (MACT) is Time on Face less delays for the 3 British pits and we have correlated it here with Time on Face less long delays, in line with the argument advanced above, for the German pits. Finally, Machine Cutting Time is a figure arrived at by calculation (Annex 3).

It must be stated that it would appear to the consultants that there is no significant difference in the productive use made of the available to cut time between the pits visited. In the period for which delay figures are available, Kellingley in England and Walsum in Germany appear to have had significantly fewer delays than the other pits visited.

It must be noted here that an improvement in the time during which the machines are cutting is possible at all pits visited and would contribute to improved productivity both in Germany and in England.

TABLE 3

This table is an attempt to compare the labour forces employed in the faces visited. It must be noted that each mine tends to have its own name for each job and these are not necessarily the same from mine to mine, let alone from country to country. In the German mines for example, each mine had a different name for the men controlling the powered supports. The English mines tended to have more standard names and these have been used as the base names.

It has therefore required an attempt by the consultants to identify those elements of the workforce common to all the faces visited—items 1 to 8 in the table. As can be seen, the actual workers on the face vary from 12 per shift at Ewald to 18 per shift at Kellingley. However, depending on the varying conditions of the face concerned, there are additional face workers required at each mine. These may be for such things as methane drainage, resin grouting, production control centres, etc. These are listed in items 11 to 17, and a total for all face workers other than maintenance men is given as item 18.

The conclusion reached is that it is almost impossible, even on a face to face basis, to establish an exact comparison of the men employed.

Engineering maintenance employees are also listed—again though, comparisons are very difficult to make.

It must be noted too that in the case of Ewald, the advance gate was being driven by conventional methods—i.e., drilling, blasting, and mucking—in conjunction with the preparation of face 5—the replacement face. The allocation of 22 men to face 4a, is therefore only a rough estimate, in fact there are more men allocated to driving both the advance gate in 4a and the new longwall 5.

In all mines there were other men in the area—but these, even including the men on the stage loader—who performed the pumping duties as well at

119

Ollerton—have been left out of this comparison as the numbers in some of the pits could not be identified.

TABLE 4   PRODUCTION STATISTICS

1. **Period**

    This table gives comparative production figures. These figures are all for different periods of time ranging from Ewald which was a relatively recently started face and for which only 9 days of production figures were available, to Kellingley and Creswell which gave us figures which enabled an average for the year to be calculated.

2. **Machine shifts per day**

    This figure was actually given by the three British mines and by Niederberg. For Walsum the figures for days worked per month and shifts worked were both given enabling this average to be calculated. For Ewald the total minutes for 9 days was given and an average time per shift, again enabling the machine shift per day to be calculated. Note that as this latter mine was on 7 hour shift times, they were able to work more than 3 shifts per day—in fact up to 5 by overlapping travelling times, but the average was 3·78.

3. **Maintenance shifts**

    All the mines claimed that the third shift, or sometimes an overlapping fourth or for Ewald fifth shift, was used for maintenance work. This does not always correlate with the figures in Table 3 for maintenance staff, i.e., full maintenance personnel are not shown for the extra shift.

4. and 5. **Advance per day/Advance per shift**

    The English pits do not normally record these figures. However, they do all give the number of strips cut and an average web. Thus the advance can be easily obtained. All the German pits conversely give these figures as a matter of routine. Only Niederberg shows a really significant difference here—due largely to the very much higher cutting rate that the shearer was able to achieve in the unique conditions.

6. **Depth of cut or web**

    This was given by all pits except Neiderberg. This oversight is not critical as it was not needed for any calculations in relation to that pit. It should be noted that the average web is not the same as the depth of the shearer drum which is normally wider than the cut taken. The depth of cut ranges from 0·51m to 0·60m and is generally a function of the total face equipment—i.e., how much coal is cut and able to be handled by the system, the shearer design and its positioning in relation to the conveyor and powered supports.

7. **Cutting rate**

    The mines were asked for an instantaneous cutting rate, i.e., at what rate can that particular shearer cut—in square metres per minute—on that particular coal face. It was hoped that this figure would have been obtained by work study as a matter of routine.

    The idea was that this cutting rate would give a measure of the potential or possible production rate achievable by that shearer in that face. In this way differences of coal hardness, dirt seams, density, etc., could be ignored as they would all be covered by the rate of cutting.

In the event, only one mine had the figure we wanted. However, in the English pits a cutting rate—an average cutting speed for each face was given. This is a standard for the pit. These are initially calculated from synthetic data—and in the case of Creswell at least, the figure was later checked by work study. The German pits did not have such a figure. However, they did record the cutting rate actually achieved during Laufzeit. On the assumption that Laufzeit in fact represents, or is intended to represent actual cutting time—the fastest time achieved per minute of Laufzeit recorded in the available figures was taken as the cutting rate for the German pits. The shortest period over which this was averaged was the 9 days at Ewald. Normally, the figure used was that for the best month. It should be noted that at Creswell, it was reported that they had, in fact, achieved the feat of cutting over one mile of coal—or say, 1,650m—in one shift. If this was taken as an average shift, they would have had to cut at a rate above the figure arrived at by work study and to have had zero delays—(which in fact they did) a cutting rate of 2·94 m²/min as against 2·76 m²/min would have been required. In all probability they did have an extended shift. However, this does indicate that the English figures, although theoretical, are probably slightly conservative and can therefore be acceptable as comparable to the ones used for Germany. It must be stressed though, that in fact the figures were arrived at through different routes for the two countries, and so comparisons based on them must be treated with caution. The cutting rates ranged from 1·87m² to 3·37 m² per minute which shows the differences of cutting rate achievable with very similar shearers due to the differing physical conditions on different faces.

8. Tonnes per shift/Tonnes per day

All the pits reported figures in this category. Unfortunately, they were reported in terms of 'saleable' tonnes. As a saleable tonne may vary from a tonne of 'clean' coal from which as much as 50 per cent of the tonnage actually mined (Ewald) has been washed, to a tonne of coal to which some ash has actually been added as required to meet specification by a customer, the tonne saleable (shown in brackets) are not much use for comparative purposes.

However, we had obtained from Kellingley, figures for tonnes of mineral removed—i.e., tonnes actually mined, and from Creswell and Ollerton figures for the density of the coal and the dirt. Since the volume of coal seam mined was known, it is possible to arrive at a reasonable figure for tonnes mined from these figures. Ewald too, gave us figures which enabled an accurate density to be calculated, and thus tonnes mined. The other two German mines required some reasonable assumptions to be made to arrive at the densities and from these and the volumes the tonnes mined were obtained. None of the German mines had immediately available for us the tonnes mined figures.

Thus these figures for tonnes per shift and tonnes per day are all, with the exception of Kellingley, calculated figures and should be treated with some caution, but are expected to be substantially correct.

121

TABLE 5

This table compares the machinery on the face. The shearers were Eickhoff in the German pits. In the UK there were two Anderson Strathclyde and one Eickhoff—the latter being specially designed to the NCB's requirements. The power of the shearers was comparable with the Germans' averaging higher power than the British. However, as can be seen by comparing the power and the cutting rate, there is not a significant correlation in that Walsum, with a very powerful shearer actually achieved a low cutting rate. Niederberg, however, with a powerful shearer, did achieve the fastest cutting rate. In general, it may be stated that it is doubtful whether for this exercise any significance can be attached to any differences in the power of the shearers, although more powerful shearers should cut faster, other factors being equal.

As far as the AFC's are concerned, again the German faces averaged out more powerful. It may be significant that Ewald, the most productive of the faces visited, also had the most powerful AFC motors. However, this is only an indication, as generally there is not much difference. It is noted though that the Germans favour double middle chain while the British seem to prefer outboard chains. We do not have the data to compare these differing units, and this comment is made merely as a note of interest.

In comparing the machines, it is clear that all are capable of producing more coal than has actually been achieved by any of the pits, if the time actually cutting can be extended.

Investigation of machine cutting time

1. English pits

1.1 *Creswell*

Reported   Shift length —330 minutes
Delays   —146·3 minutes
MATC   —183·7 minutes
               161· minutes—Standard Machine Running Time

Face length —268 m. Strips per shift 1·97
Advance per
shift   —1·143m.   Web 0·58m therefore distance travelled 528m.

Therefore, area shearer cut per shift 306·3m² (Note that in one shift a record of some 1,670 linear metres (969m² assuming 0·58 web) was actually cut.

Now from other figures given, it has been calculated that when the machine is cutting at Creswell it should cut at a rate of 2·76 metres² per minute.

On this assumption the machine would have been operative, actually cutting for (MCT) 111 minutes per shift, or 60% of MATC and 34% of Time on Face.

Alternatively, if the 161 minutes is accepted the machine must only have achieved 1·902 metres per minute.

1.2 *Ollerton*

Reported   Shift length —326 min.
Delays   —105 min.
MATC   —221 min.
               160 minutes—Standard Machine Running Time.

Face length —259m.
Advance per
shift   —1·385m.

Therefore, area shearer cuts—294·8 m².
Machine cutting rate should be 1·969 metres²/min.
Therefore the machine would actually be cutting for (MCT) 149·75 minutes per shift—which is 66% of MATC and 45% of Time on Face.

1.3 *Kellingley*

Reported   Shift length —321 min.
Delays   —51·4 min.
MATC   —263·4 min.
Face length —230m.
Advance per
shift   —1·414m.

Therefore, area shearer cuts—325·22 m²

Machine cutting rate should be 2·086 m²/min.

Therefore the machine would actually be cutting for (MCT) 155·9 minutes per shift—which is 59% of MATC and 49% of Time on Face.

2. German Pits

2.1 *Niederberg*

Reported Shift length —337 min.

Delays   —   —

MATC   —   —Laufzeit 161·2

Face length —200m.

Advance

per Shift   —2·42m.

Therefore, area shearer cuts—484 m²/shift

Machine cutting rate 3·37 m²/min.

Therefore Machine cutting time (MCT) 143·6 minutes per shift which is 66% of MATC and 43% of TOF.

2.2 *Ewald*

Reported Shift length —286m.

Delays   —162m.

Laufzeit   —124m.

Face length —261m.

Advance per

shift   —1·32m.

The shearer cuts 344·52 m²/shift

Therefore the machine cutting rate (best month) 2·73m²/min. (The Germans gave no standard)

Therefore the machine would actually be cutting for 126·2 minutes per shift—which is 56% of MATC and 44% of Time on Face.

2.3 *Walsum*

Reported Shift length —334m.

Delays   —118·6m.

Laufzeit   —215·4m.

Face length —272m.

Face advance

per shift   —1·29m.

Therefore the shearer cuts 350·88 m²/shift

Machine cutting rate 1·87 (best month)

Therefore Machine cutting time 188 minutes—which is 75% of MATC and 56% of Time on Face.

APPENDIX 7.2
(referred to in paragraph 7.92)

Areas and collieries visited to study labour efficiency

South Nottinghamshire Area

Bentinck
Calverton
Cotgrave

North Derbyshire Area

Bolsover
Shirebrook

Doncaster Area

Scottish Area

Welsh Area

The Board's scheme of allowances for long distance transferred industrial staff

Preliminary visit to new location

1. Not more than two days pay during the period of notice to visit his proposed new colliery and be interviewed by management there. If an offer of employment is made and accepted arrangements can be made (usually after termination of employment) for the transferee to visit the new location for up to five days for the purpose of looking at housing, schools, etc. In both instances the cost of transport and subsistence for both the man and his wife are paid.

Fares and subsistence

2. The cost of fares and subsistence when the transferee and his family moved to their new location, and of weekly travel to the former home district (while the man is in receipt of lodging allowance).

Make-up of lost wages

3. Transferees who unavoidably lose working time in travelling to the place of new employment are reimbursed for the working time lost.

Disturbance allowance

4. An allowance of £2,000 paid when the transferee has taken up his new employment.

Settling-in allowance

5. Transferees without dependants receive an allowance equivalent to Class C Rate II subsistence (as published in the Board's rules for travelling, subsistence etc for non-industrial staff) for the first 28 days following arrival at the new place of employment.

Lodging allowance

6. This allowance is paid to transferees with dependants awaiting permanent accommodation at the new location as follows:

   first 28 nights—Class C Rate II subsistence per night
   next six months—Cost of accommodation up to a maximum of Class C Rate II subsistence per night.

   For transferees under age 18 without dependants the full cost of lodgings is met subject to a contribution deducted from the transferee's wages.

Removal expenses

7. The cost of removal expenses including insurance, subject to obtaining at least two estimates.

Household settlement grant

8. Transferees with dependants are eligible for a grant equivalent to the Class C household settlement grant paid to non-industrial staff payable as soon as the transferee moves into a house in the new location.

Continuing liability allowance

9. When the dependants of a transferee join him and the transferee is still liable for rent, storage of furniture etc in the old district, the cost of such unavoidable commitments is met for a period of three months, subject to review at monthly intervals.

Increased rent allowance

10. If a transferee with dependants has to pay more by way of rent or mortagage repayments in the new district than he was paying in his old location he normally receives the whole of the difference for the first four years, 75 per cent in the fifth year, 50 per cent in the sixth year and 25 per cent in the seventh.

House sale or purchase grant

11. Reimbursement of the reasonable cost of house agents' and solicitors' fees necessarily incurred on the sale of a house in the old district and/or purchase of a house in the new district. The reasonable costs of a structural survey and a test of drains of a house in the new location are also reimbursed.

The Board's scheme of allowance for long distance transferred non-industrial staff

The allowances in this annex apply equally to married and single, male and female Board staff unless otherwise stated.

Long distance transfer scheme

1. A taxable payment of £1,550 paid in the case of compulsory transfer as a result of closure, relocation or reorganisation of a Board activity.

Preliminary visit to new location

2. Up to 5 days special paid leave to visit new location and house hunt etc. Expenses for transferee and spouse are met for up to four nights.

3. Travel and subsistence expenses for transferee and family to take up new posts.

Lodging allowance

4. For staff unable to find permanent accommodation on transfer the Board meet reasonable lodging expenses necessarily incurred for a maximum period of 7 months.

Weekly fares home

5. Paid in a period of lodging allowance until transferee is joined by his family.

House sale and purchase assistance

The Board reimburse reasonable

6. Legal fees

7. Estate agent fees

8. Cost of independent survey

9. Cost of test of drains

10. Furniture removal expenses

11. Telephone installation charge where appropriate.

Household Settlement Grant

12. The Board pay the following allowances to contribute towards the miscellaneous expenses incurred in removal, curtains, carpets, etc.

	Married staff	Single staff
A.	£1,170	£680
B.	£1,030	£625

Excess rent allowance

13. An allowance paid for seven years, in full for three years and reducing in the following four years to nil to help with any increase in housing costs. The allowance is subject to an annual maximum of £975 (£1,240 in London).

Guaranteed valuation scheme

14. The scheme is designed to help staff sell the house at the old location at a price not below that of an independent valuation reserve figure. The objective is to ensure that the individual receives at least the independent valuation reserve figure on the sale of his house. The Board will make up the difference where the highest offer falls below the independent valuation reserve figure.

Overlapping property expenses

15. Where a transferee has to purchase a property at the new location before he has disposed of his property at the old location, the Board will reimburse the net interest paid on any mortgage loan on the property at the old location and the interest charged on that part of the money from the delayed sale which he is unable to offset against the loan on the new property. Overlapping interest is normally paid for a period of six months or where the individual has entered the guaranteed valuation scheme, until he has disposed of the property at the old station.

128

Enhancement of benefits under the Redundant Mineworkers' Payments Scheme and the Mineworkers' Pension Scheme and payments to industrial employees transferring within daily travelling distance of home

1. The Government decided to extend the benefits paid under the Redundant Mineworkers' Payments Scheme for men whose date of redundancy falls on or after 11 March 1981. An Order (SI 1981 No 482) providing for payment of these increased benefits was made on 25 March 1981.

2. The National Coal Board and Government decided that allowances for short distance transferees should also be increased.

3. The Board also proposed to the National Union of Mineworkers possible amendments to the Mineworkers' Pension Scheme to enhance the benefits payable to men who are made redundant. What has been agreed is set out in paragraph 12 below.

Redundant Mineworkers' Payments Scheme—Enhanced benefits

A. Lump sums

Men aged 21 to 29

4. An additional lump sum of £100 at age 21 increasing by £100 for each additional year of age to £900 at age 29 at date of redundancy.

Men aged 30 to 49

5. An additional lump sum payment of £1,000 for those aged 30 to 39, £1,500 for those aged 40 to 49 at date of redundancy.

Men aged 50 to 54

6. An additional lump sum payment equal to twice their Employment Protection (Consolidation) Act lump sum entitlement to redundant persons aged 50 to 54 at date of redundancy.

Men aged 55 to 59

7. A lump sum payment based on their Employment Protection (Consolidation) Act lump sum entitlement is paid to redundant persons aged 55 to 59 who at date of redundancy are entitled to receive weekly payments (or a lump sum if they do not have at least 10 years service in the industry to qualify for weekly benefits) under the Redundant Mineworkers' Payment Scheme. The amount of the supplementary lump sum payment as a percentage of the EP(C)A entitlement is 200 per cent for a beneficiary aged 55 at date of redundancy, 150 per cent at age 56, 100 per cent at age 57, 75 per cent at age 58 and 50 per cent at age 59.

B. Extension to weekly benefit

8. Under the terms of the former Redundant Mineworkers Payments Scheme basic benefit was payable to men aged 55 to 64 for a period of 156 weeks from the date of redundancy or to age 65 (women 60) or date of death, whichever was the earliest.

9. The Scheme has been amended to extend the 156 week period by a further period of 104 weeks to 260 weeks or to age 65 (women 60) or date of death, whichever is the earliest.

Changes to earnings levels etc

10. The Order provided for a new table of basic weekly benefits for men made redundant on or after 6 April 1981 which raised the ceiling on earnings taken into account for calculating RMPS benefit from £120 to £130 per week. The Order also made provision for adjustments to other benefit qualifications.

Payments to industrial employees transferred within daily travelling distance of home

11. The amounts of transfer and retention payments have been increased in accordance with the following table:

Length of continuous service	Initial transfer payment on taking up employment at new location £	Subsequent retention payments after		
		6 months £	12 months £	24 months £
Under 2 years	250	250	250	250
2 years—under 5 years	500	250	250	250
5 years—under 10 years	600	250	250	250
10 years and over	800	250	250	250

Mineworkers' pension scheme

12. The Board and the National Union of Mineworkers have improved Mineworkers' Pension Scheme benefits for miners made redundant when aged between 50 and 59. Mineworkers aged 55 to 59 at date of redundancy formerly started to draw their MPS pensions after the three year period of RMPS basic benefits. The three years has now become five years; but provided they have 10 years' qualifying service the pension has been improved by giving free credit for the period of contributing service that they would have served if they had stayed on to age 60. This improved pension is payable for life. For mineworkers aged 50 to 54 at date of redundancy not only is their MPS pension paid immediately on redundancy (they formerly had to wait until age 65), but provided they have 10 years' qualifying service they also get free credit of five years' service.

13. The attached table indicates some examples of the enhanced benefits payable under the RMPS and the MPS.

TABLE 1 Schedule indicating benefits paid to redundant mineworkers based on average earnings of £130 per week

		Redundant Mineworkers' Payment Scheme									Mineworkers' Pension Scheme — After enhancement			
Age	Years of service	Payment under EP(C)A	Supplementary lump sum to age 49	Supplementary lump sum age 50 to 59 — % of col 3	Amount	Existing lump sums	Weekly benefits (see Note 3) — 5 year basic	UBE only	Total redundancy benefits	Increase on former entitlement	Extra 90ths	Lump sum	Pension	Total benefits (col 10+13+14)
1	2	3	4	5	6	7	8	9	10	11	12	13	14	15
		£	£		£	£	£	£	£	£	£	£	£	£
21	2	130	100	—	—	65	—	—	295	100	—	—	—	295
29	9	1,040	900	—	—	585	—	—	2,525	900	—	—	—	2,525
30	10	1,170	1,000	—	—	650	—	—	2,820	1,000	—	—	—	2,820
35	15	1,820	1,000	—	—	1,560	—	—	4,380	1,000	—	—	—	4,380
39	19	2,340	1,000	—	—	2,470	—	—	5,810	1,000	—	—	—	5,810
40	20	2,470	1,500	—	—	2,600	—	—	6,570	1,500	—	—	—	6,570
45	25	2,860	1,500	—	—	4,225	—	—	8,585	1,500	—	—	—	8,585
50	30	3,185	—	200	6,370	5,850	—	—	15,405	6,370	5	2,496	12,480	30,381
54	34	3,445	—	200	6,890	6,630	—	—	16,965	6,890	5	2,496	9,152	28,613
55	35	3,510	—	200	7,020	—	18,207	6,744	35,481	11,373	5	2,496	4,160	42,137
56	36	3,575	—	150	5,363	—	18,207	5,396	32,541	9,808	4	2,340	3,120	38,001
57	37	3,640	—	100	3,640	—	18,207	4,047	29,534	8,176	3	2,028	2,028	33,590
58	38	3,705	—	75	2,778	—	18,207	2,698	27,388	7,405	2	1,872	1,248	30,508
59	39	3,770	—	50	1,885	—	18,207	1,349	25,211	6,603	1	1,560	520	27,291
60	40	3,835	—	—	—	—	18,207	—	22,042	4,808	—	—	—	22,042
61	41	3,900	—	—	—	—	14,222	—	18,122	2,263	—	—	—	18,122
62	42	3,900	—	—	—	—	10,519	—	14,419	—	—	—	—	14,419
63	43	3,900	—	—	—	—	6,434	—	10,334	—	—	—	—	10,334
64	44	3,900	—	—	—	—	2,350	—	6,250	—	—	—	—	6,250

Notes: (1) Based on maximum of £130 per week permitted up to February 1982 for purposes of entitlement under the Employment Protection (Consolidation) Act—column 3.

(2) MPS benefits (columns 13 and 14) are based on an average pension of £9.00 per week being increased up to £16.00 per week after the addition of the extra 90ths shown. The MPS lump sums shown are payable in the case of the redundant at age 50 and 54 immediately and for the 55 year old, after the 5 years RMPS basic weekly benefit period.

(3) The amounts shown in columns 8 and 9 assume that the beneficiary remains unemployed up to age 65.

Source: The NCB.

Appendix 9.1

(referred to in paragraph 9.15)

Approval at Headquarters of investment in projects at Stage II

(1)	(2)	(3)	(4)	(5)	(6)
Activity	(A) Head of the appropriate Headquarters department or person directly responsible for the activity or department (shown at A below) with the concurrence of (B) the appropriate representative of Headquarters Finance Department (shown at B below).	(A) Director General of Finance and (B) Head of the appropriate Headquarters department. Director of the establishment. Chairman of the executive or head of formation (shown at B below), subject to the concurrence of (C) the head of any other Headquarters department functionally concerned.	(A) Board member for Finance and (B) Board member with a particular interest in the affairs of the appropriate department, establishment, executive or other formation (or the Deputy Chairman where there is no such Board member) (shown at B below), on the recommendation of (C) Director General of Finance and (D) Head of the appropriate Headquarters department. Director of establishment, managing director or general manager of the executive or Head of the formation as appropriate (shown at D below), subject to the concurrence of (E) the Head of any other Headquarters department functionally concerned.	Mining Committee	General Purposes Committee
1. Collieries (excluding offices, for which see item 2 below). Including interim Stage III	A: D G of Mining B: Deputy D G of Finance	£50,000	£500,000	No limit (except that the Chairman of the Board in consultation with the Chairman of the Mining Committee may consider whether projects costing over £5m which raise important issues—for example, those which would need to be referred to the Department of Energy for their comments—should be referred to the General Purposes Committee).	No limit
		B: D G of Mining	£1m		
			B: Board member for Mining D: D G of Mining		

	£50,000	£250,000	£500,000		No limit
				£1m	No limit
2. Other Area activities (excluding land for operational purposes, for which see item 1 above)	A: Head of department etc B: Deputy D G of Finance	B: Head of department etc	B: Appropriate Board member or Deputy Chairman		
3. Opencast Executive	—		£1m B: Chairman of Opencast Executive D: Managing Director of Opencast Executive	£5m	No limit
4. MRDE	—	B: Director at MRDE	B: Board member for Mining D: Director at MRDE	£5m	No limit
5. CRE	—	B: Director of CRE	B: Director of CRE* D: Director of CRE	—	No limit
6. Minestone Executive	—	B: General Manager of Minestone Executive	B: Chairman of Minestone Executive D: General Manager of Minestone Executive	—	No limit
7. Headquarters departments (including regional activities): Operational Research Executive, Institute of Occupational Medicine etc	A: Head of department director of CRE or of ICM etc B: Appropriate representative of Finance Department	B: Head of department etc	B: Appropriate Board Member or Deputy Chairman D: Head of department	—	No limit

Amounts shown in cells: row 2 — £50,000 / £250,000 / £500,000; rows 4–7 — £250,000 / £500,000; row 7 left column — £250,000.

*Second Annex No 26 to MC/M(31)12
Item G4 refers (paragraph xiii)

The Thorne colliery project

Background to the project

1. Thorne colliery (opened in 1926) was closed in 1956 as a result of continuing problems of seepage of water into the shafts. In 1967 Doncaster Area submitted Stage I proposals for reopening the colliery but the Board decided to keep the colliery on a 'care and maintenance' basis because demand for coal was falling. Since then a number of proposals, both for closing and reopening Thorne, have been considered. In 1974, following Plan for Coal and the improvement in market prospects, it was realised that in view of the requirement for new capacity, the reopening of Thorne held considerable advantages in that access existed and, hence, it could be brought into production more quickly than a greenfield new mine site. A further substantial advantage in the case of Thorne was that reconstruction would not be delayed by having to go through planning application procedures.

2. Impetus to the reopening of Thorne was provided by a formal request by the NUM in 1975 for the reopening and pressure from Members of Parliament. A paper was presented to the Mining Committee by the Area Director and it was agreed that a feasibility study should be prepared. In January 1976 a feasibility/Stage I study was submitted and subsequently Thorne was included in the National Exploration Programme. Six surface boreholes were put down and proved excellent sections of High Hazel seam and extensive areas of Barnsley seam. In January 1977 the Area was requested to submit Stage I proposals and these were completed in March 1977.

Nature and main objectives of the project

3. The Area proposed to retain and refurbish the two existing shafts and sink a new shaft to the same depth to operate as the main coal winding shaft. The surface area was to be rebuilt completely and a new pit bottom was to be established. The initial objective at Stage I was to achieve an annual output level of 500,000 tons within five years (Phase 1) and 1·6 million tons by year eight (Phase 2) although the aim was to equip and engineer the colliery for an annual rate of production equivalent to approximately 2 million tons.

Stage I

4. The Area submission examined four alternative methods of reopening Thorne:

   (*a*) utilising the existing shafts and pit bottom;

   (*b*) utilising the existing shafts and forming a new pit bottom;

   (*c*) the Area proposal summarised in paragraph 3 above; and

   (*d*) a combination of (*c*) and (*a*), that is commissioning the existing shafts in advance of the completion of No 3 shaft.

5. The Area rejected the first two alternatives because of the restriction on output which would be imposed by the narrow shaft diameters and because of the risk of relying on two shafts which had a history of geological problems associated with them. The final alternative was rejected because it would delay the completion of Phase 1 of the project.

6. The Area's proposal was estimated to cost £86·4 million at February 1977 price levels; this included the cost of a multi-product coal preparation plant. The results of the investment were projected to be an annual output of 1·56 million tons based on estimates of face OMS of 20·61 tons and overall OMS of 5·78 tons.

7. The financial appraisal of the Area's proposal, over a 20 year period of full output, projected a DCF yield of 11·5 per cent on the basis of constant prices and costs. Headquarters Finance Department thought that the capital cost was under-estimated by £12 million; it also pointed out that the level of productivity postulated in the proposal was some 60 per cent more than the best level achieved over a sustained period at other collieries in the Area and three times higher than that achieved in two neighbouring collieries.

8. The Finance Department's DCF appraisal of the revised capital estimate was carried out both on the basis of constant prices and costs and on real price and wages costs assumptions. It assumed that proceeds would be equivalent to 10·5p per therm to 1985–86, and would grow at 2·75 per cent per annum in real terms thereafter until the year 2000. Operating costs were assumed to increase at a slower rate over the period. The table below summarises the projected DCF yields before and after risk.

	Current price levels	Taking account of real increases in selling prices + wages costs
	%	%
Base case: no risk, project cost £98 million	10	15
Base case taking account of risk:		
(a) shortfall in output:		
(i) 10 per cent	7	12
(ii) 20 per cent	4	9
(b) capital cost:		
increase of 10 per cent	9	14
(c) delay in scheme completion:		
1 year	9	14
Cumulative effect of (a)(ii)+(b)+(c)	3	7

9. The Mining Department considered that the project was more likely to cost £110 to £120 million and emphasised the importance of achieving the design potential of the pit, namely 2 million tons.

10. The Board paper (May 1977) recommended, *inter alia,* that the Area should prepare a Stage II submission within a year for the reopening of Thorne colliery with an annual output on completion of Phase 2 of 2 million tons; Interim Stage III authority be given for the expenditure of £1·2 million at February 1977 prices on several items including general

expenses, site access and service, temporary power supply, a hydrogeological borehole and shaft refurbishment.

Interim Stage III applications for capital expenditure prior to the Stage I Plus submission

11. In August 1977 a further £260,000 was authorised under Interim Stage III procedures, for the employment of consultants and quantity surveyors to assist with the planning of the project. In February 1978 the Area submitted an application for £3·9 million which was discussed by the Mining Committee in April. This concerned the proposed installation of winding engines for Nos 1 and 2 shafts. The Mining Committee referred this interim application to the General Purposes Committee and asked for a paper which included:

   (a) the costs and consequences (including delays) of not approving at this stage the Interim Stage III application on the assumption that the Board did subsequently agree to re-open Thorne;

   (b) the total abortive expenditure likely to be incurred if the Interim Stage III approval was granted and the Board decided subsequently not to re-open Thorne; and

   (c) the total costs (and potential abortive expenditure) of any further Interim Stage III approvals likely to be sought in advance of a formal decision in principle being taken by the Board to re-open Thorne.

   Of the revised £3·7 million estimate, £553,500 was considered to be non-recoverable in the event of the Board rejecting the Stage II proposal and it was estimated that to await the Stage II submission in November would set the whole programme back by 12 months. In May 1978 the General Purposes Committee granted the Interim Stage III authority and requested that a Stage I Plus submission be put to them by September. It also agreed that in the meantime no further Interim Stage III authorisation should be granted.

12. In September 1978 Interim Stage III authority was given for a further £246,000 expenditure for consultants' and quantity surveyors' fees to the end of March 1979.

Stage I Plus

13. The Area submitted its Stage I Plus proposals in November 1978. The Area's estimate of the cost had increased to £177·8 million (including £15·7 million for plant pool equipment) at September 1978 prices. Allowing for inflation, this represented an increase in the estimate of cost between Stage I and Stage I Plus of £75 million. The Board paper explained that the increase in the estimate of cost reflected the more precisely costed design now available, together with technical changes resulting directly from the increase in projected saleable output from 1·5 million tonnes per annum to 2·0 million tonnes per annum.

14. The total manpower requirement for the colliery in the first year of full output was estimated to be 1,450. Face OMS was estimated to be 27·62 tonnes and overall OMS 7·29 tonnes. Headquarters Industrial Relations

136

Department and the Area were in agreement that, provided the staffing of the colliery was carefully planned, the potential risks of a shortfall in manpower could be overcome.

15. The Area estimated that, of the 2 million tonnes output, 73 per cent would be sold to the electricity market, 16 per cent to the industrial market and 11 per cent to the domestic market. Average proceeds at October 1978 prices were projected to be £23·8 per tonne and operating costs £16·98, producing an operating profit before interest of £6·82 per tonne. The project was expected to yield a DCF return of 8 per cent over a 47 year period and 7 per cent over a 30 year period, assuming constant prices and costs.

16. In the Board paper, the Mining Department considered that the cost of the project could be reduced and that an annual saleable output of 2·14 million tonnes could be achieved. It considered that the high productivity performance could be achieved (and was being achieved elsewhere) with the high standard of engineering provided in a new mine.

17. The financial appraisal was projected over a period of 30 years and 47 years because the reserves assessment would support such a timescale. Both constant and real price assumptions were considered. As in Stage I the financial appraisal in real price terms assumed that proceeds would rise faster than unit operating costs over the appraisal period. The paper identified two risks inherent in the investment proposal as being crucial to its success: the most important was the risk of failing to achieve in full the productivity levels postulated in the submission; the second was the risk of delay. The results of the appraisal and the risk analysis according to constant and real price assumptions over a 30 year and 47 year appraisal period are summarised below.

	DCF yield (%)	
	At current prices	At real price
(i) *Over 30 years*		
(a) Base case	7	12
Base case adjusted for:		
(b) Shortfall in output of 20 per cent	2	8
(c) Increase in project cost: by 10 per cent	6	11
(d) : for delay of 1 year	6	11
(e) Delay in project completion by 1 year	6	11
(f) Pessimistic case, ie (b)+(c)+(d)+(e)	NIL	6
Output shortfall to still give 5 per cent DCF yield (output only risk)	8	28
(ii) *Over 47 years*		
(a) Base case	8	13
Base case adjusted for:		
(b) Shortfall in output of 20 per cent	4	9
(c) Increase in project cost: by 10 per cent	7	12
(d) : for delay of 1 year	7	12
(e) Delay in project completion by 1 year	8	12
(f) Pessimistic case, ie (b)+(c)+(d)+(e)	3	8
Output shortfall to still give 5 per cent DCF yield (output only risk)	14	37

18. The Board paper observed that for the pessimistic case, the assumption of rising real prices, the project would yield a return in excess of the 5 per cent required rate of return, but that there was virtually no return on the investment under the constant price assumption after allowing for the same measure of risk. The Central Planning Unit advised that in view of the high productivity being postulated the Board should consider seeking assurances in the form of improved performances in the Doncaster Area before entering into further major commitments on the project.

19. The Board paper also considered the Area's Interim Stage III applications for expenditures amounting to £8·6 million, to maintain the continuity of the project. These were detailed as follows:

No 5 Interim Stage III (£5,247,088): Including £2 million to enable the NCB team, consultants, quantity surveyors and the colliery to operate for a further 12 months. The remainder required to make a commitment on long-term items, namely £50,000 for diversion of an oil pipeline; £1,625,348 to order Nos 1 and 2 headgears and foundations; £74,416 to order Nos 1 and 2 shaft signals; and £1·5 million for initial commitment on the freezing plant and associated works at No 3 shaft.

Note: Recoverable £74,416 on shaft signals
Non-recoverable £5·17 million

No 6 Interim Stage III (£1,889,277): Including £1·6 million for recovery of Nos 1 and 2 shaft sumps; £126,000 for temporary ventilation; and £168,000 for demolition, mainly of reinforced concrete gantries.

Note: Recoverable £50,000 on ventilation equipment
Non-recoverable £1·84 million

No 7 Interim Stage III (£1,459,200): To permit work to commence on establishing new insets at Nos 1 and 2 shafts.

Note: All expenditure would be non-recoverable.

20. The General Purposes Committee discussed the proposal on 19 January 1979. The Committee gave approval to the scheme in principle and asked the Secretary to inform the Department of Energy of the progress of the project; it requested the Area to prepare a Stage II submission based on an annual saleable output of 2·1 million tonnes. It also requested the Area Director to negotiate a memorandum of understanding with the unions locally to achieve the best performance possible at the colliery and to assist in recruitment; close liaison with headquarters was to be maintained to ensure that the forecast levels of performance were achieved. The Committee approved the Interim Stage III applications.

Interim Stage III application prior to the Stage II submission

21. The Area submitted a further application for capital in October 1979 amounting to £22·5 million; this included some £13 million for the sinking of the No 3 shaft. Following investigation by the Mining Department the Area agreed to delete this part of the application on the basis that the Stage II proposals would be available for consideration by March 1980. The £6·4 million which formed the revised application was mainly required for

surface drainage and for shaft and mine equipment at Nos 1 and 2 shafts, so as to provide access to the mine and facilities for pit bottom work. The Mining Committee discussed the application on 20 December 1979 and granted the Area authority for the £6·4 million expenditure.

Stage II proposals submission

22. The Area submitted the Stage II proposals in January 1980. The main technical proposals were basically the same as those presented in the Stage I Plus submission. Discussions between Area and headquarters following Stage I Plus resulted in cost reductions of £9·3 million but these were largely offset by design changes and other increases of £6·9 million. The total cost of the project at December 1979 prices was projected to be £211·7 million, including the cost of plant pool equipment (£17·3 million).

23. As requested by the General Purposes Committee planned output was increased to 2·1 million tonnes which, with the same level of manpower required, resulted in a small increase in OMS. Estimates of OMS comparable with the Stage I Plus figures would be a face OMS of 28·98 tonnes and overall OMS of 7·66 tonnes. The estimated results of the project, based on prices prevailing in December 1979, are summarised in the table below. This shows the Area estimate of face OMS to be 40·97 tonnes, the apparent improvement being due to a national change in the definition of face shifts.

First full year of output		1987—88	
Saleable output (m tonnes)		2·1	
OMS (tonnes): face		40·97	
overall		7·66	
Average manpower		1,450	
	£'000		£/tonne
Proceeds	62,213		29·63
Operating costs	40,826		19·45
Profit/(loss): before interest	21,387		10·18
after interest	(15,274)		(7·28)
Net cash flow		+£894·8m	
NPV (discounted at 10 per cent)		+£4·0m	
Undiscounted pay back		Year 14	

24. The Stage II submission adopted the 47 year appraisal period that had been used in the Stage I Plus submission, and similar allowances for risk were also adopted. However, the assumption relating to the real increase in prices was revised downwards from that in the Stage I Plus. Nevertheless, as can be seen below, the DCF yield in real terms remained higher than the yield based on current price assumptions. The Board paper provided the following summary of results.

	DCF yield (%)	
	Current prices	Real prices
Base case	10	15
Base case adjusted for:		
(a) a 20 per cent shortfall in output	6	11
(b) a 10 per cent increase in project cost	9	14
(c) a one year's delay in project completion	9	14
(d) Pessimistic case, ie (a)+(b)+(c)	5	10

25. The General Purposes Committee gave its approval at a meeting on 21 March 1980; the Area was formally notified on 9 April 1980.

(referred to in paragraphs 9.55 and 10.1)

Grimethorpe South Side project

Nature and main objectives of the project

1. The project is to concentrate the outputs from the Grimethorpe, Houghton Main, Barrow and, Darfield Main collieries to a common coal preparation plant via a new surface drift and to rapid loading despatch points
   located on Grimethorpe surface. It includes underground connections
   between the four collieries with conveyor transport bringing the output to
   the new surface drift.

2. The project which was designed to increase output and productivity, was
   estimated to cost £112·3 million at 1979 price levels, and is scheduled to be
   completed during the four year period from 1979–80 to 1982–83. It
   includes the consolidation of two former schemes, one for the rehabilitation of Barnsely Main and one involving surface drift arrangements for
   Grimethorpe and Houghton Main only.

3. At 31 March 1980 the net book value of fixed assets in the Barnsley Area
   was £138·3 million (at historical cost and after the capital reconstructions
   in 1965–66 and 1972–73), and this project was therefore of considerable
   importance in relation to the overall level of investment in the Area. As a
   result of the scheme, total saleable output from the four collieries involved
   was projected to increase from 2·3 million tonnes to 2·9 million tonnes,
   while a further 0·5 million tonnes was to be derived from the (separate)
   Houghton Dunsil project. This compared with a total for the Barnsley
   Area in 1979–80 of 8·1 million tonnes. Average output per man-shift
   (OMS) in the Area was 2·56 tonnes at the start of the project and the
   average of the four collieries was 2·05 tonnes. The scheme was designed to
   increase this average to 3·37 tonnes.

4. The combined loss of the four collieries in 1978–79 amounted to £5·9
   million after interest charges. In 1983–84, the year following completion
   of the project, the profit after interest charges was projected to be £5·6
   million.

Background to the project: Area and regional objectives

5. Barnsley Area has traditionally been an important supplier of coking coal.
   In 1970 Area officials realised that output and profitability had reached a
   plateau, and at that time four main objectives were defined:
   - (*a*) to achieve at least 8 million tonnes per annum total output with
     reduced manpower and increased efficiency and productivity;
   - (*b*) to reduce the number of despatch points;
   - (*c*) to substitute new efficient mines for old exhausted mines; and
   - (*d*) to improve the quality and flexibility of coal preparation plants to
     meet fluctuations in market demand.

6. Since 1974, the NCB has evaluated the plans and investment proposals for the production of coking coal in the Barnsley Area within a wider strategy encompassing the entire Yorkshire coalfield. In 1974 the NCB identified a potential shortage of coking-coal capacity developing across the Region. Various options including the Grimethorpe complex were considered for meeting the projected demand under the 'Yorkshire Coking Coal Strategy'.

Stage I

7. The Stage I submission was made by the Barnsley Area on 25 August 1978. The proposal at this stage was to construct a new zig-zag surface drift at Grimethorpe colliery at a cost of £13·2 million and to convey in separate streams the Grimethorpe upper seams and the combined output from the Grimethorpe and Houghton Main lower seams. The submission, however, had been prepared in the light of a large project for Grimethorpe which included the raising, preparation and despatching of output from two other adjacent collieries, Barrow and Darfield Main. This project had been discussed with Headquarters staff and the Stage I proposals had been designed to be compatible with the wider scheme if the Board wished to examine it further.

8. The objectives of the original scheme were stated in the submission to be: to remove shaft capacity constraints on output from the lower seams, to minimise the need for Markham equipment in the shafts, to save manpower, to separate the output of the upper and lower seams and to improve facilities for preparation of the output.

9. Two alternatives to the proposed scheme were considered:

   (a) retaining the present winding system—this was rejected because it would provide no long-term solution to shaft capacity constraints and represented a less efficient method of winding coal which required separate preparation; and

   (b) constructing a surface drift for lower seams only—this was rejected to allow elimination of coal winding at both shafts.

10. The submission provided a brief history of each colliery and set out the financial results of each from 1973 to the first three months of 1978–79. It also provided an analysis of the coal reserves at the two collieries and commented on the characteristics of each seam. As a result of the schemes removing the constraint on shaft capacity it was estimated that output would increase by 235,000 tonnes per annum to 1,956,000 tonnes. The incremental benefits of eliminating the shaft bottleneck were appraised against the project cost and additional costs of production. The DCF calculations in the Stage I submission indicated that the net present value (NPV) of the project over a 15 year appraisal period was £15·255 million, using a discount rate of 10 per cent. Various risk factors were considered including a 20 per cent increase in project costs, a reduction in incremental proceeds of 10 per cent and washed coking smalls being sold to the electricity market. It was estimated that the project would remain viable for each eventuality and that the projects would still break even if incremental output reduced by 63 per cent.

141

11. By the time the Stage I proposals were formally discussed by the Mining Committee, on 26 October 1978, it had been decided that the Area should prepare a Stage II submission incorporating the wider proposals. But in view of the high prospective marginal returns of the smaller surface drift project, which was in any case compatible with the larger proposals, the Mining Committee granted the Area interim Stage III authority to spend £993,000 at July 1978 prices in respect of the surface drift project, most of which concerned work on the surface drift portal and 300 metres drivage of the first leg of the drift.

12. Further interim Stage III authority was granted on 7 February 1979 for expenditure of £950,000 on the rehabilitation of Barnsley Main No 4 shaft in order to ensure the safety of the mine and improve machine available time. In October 1979 an application for interim Stage III authority to spend £480,000 on initial work to deepen Darfield No 3 shaft was submitted but not processed.

Stage II

13. The nature, objectives and main effects of the project have been summarised above.

Alternatives

14. The main alternative to the scheme was not to concentrate output at Grimethorpe colliery but to undertake separate investment at the four collieries instead; this was known as the 'do nothing' situation. The extent of the investment required in the 'do nothing' situation was influenced by four important factors:

(a) The age and condition of the existing CPP facilities at Barrow, Darfield and Grimethorpe.

(b) At Darfield Main the development of the deeper Silkstone seam reserves was essential if continuity of production were to be maintained. This seam which was high quality coal formed over 50 per cent of colliery reserves; it offered good working conditions but the thickness of the seam was only 85–93cms.

(c) The future of Barrow was dependent upon the exploitation of the thicker and more productive Parkgate and Fenton seam reserves situated some way north of Barrow.

(d) The Grimethorpe surface drift was committed (unless authority for the longer straight drift which formed the Stage II submission was given) and its completion would result in additional output being raised at Grimethorpe, which would require new facilities to handle the prospective level of output.

142

15. Acceptance of all three necessitated 'do nothing' expenditure of between £90 million and £100 million as follows:

		£m
(a)	New coal preparation plant (CPP) at Barrow due to the age and condition of the present plant	9
(b)	Improvements to the CPP at Darfield	4
(c)	Accessing the Silkstone seam at Darfield to replace exhausting reserves in the Kents Thick seam	16
(d)	Rehabilitating No 4 shaft at Barnsley Main to allow the thicker Parkgate and Fenton seams to be developed and to improve MAT	14
(e)	Completion of the drift at Grimethorpe to remove winding restrictions at the lower level	11
(f)	New CPP and peripherals at Grimethorpe due to the age and condition of the existing plant	37–46
		91–100

16. The Board was advised that decisions about the future of Darfield Main and Barrow had to be made in the wider Yorkshire context because of the local union structure and in view of that it was thought the two collieries would not be suitable candidates for closure. The Board was advised of the need for a new CPP at Grimethorpe because the present plant was 18 years old and subject to increasing operating costs.

17. Other alterations to achieve the Area's objective of concentration of outputs to a comon point were also considered. They included:

(a) Concentration of winding and coal preparation at either Barrow, Darfield Main or Houghton Main; this was rejected because it was evident that to concentrate output and preparation at any colliery other than Grimethorpe would involve greater investment and higher operating costs.

(b) Transport of output to Grimethorpe by road; this was rejected because it involved carrying 6,400 tonnes per day through built-up areas and because the total output of the scheme would be lower than the surface drift scheme.

(c) Improved shaft winding at Grimethorpe to wind the total combined output; this required an additional shaft at Grimethorpe which would cost as much as the proposed drift and would be more expensive to operate.

(d) Driving the smaller 'zig-zag' drift at Grimethorpe and developing Barrow and Darfield Main as necessary. The Board was advised that, while the smaller project would achieve the results at Grimethorpe and Houghton Main, the overall cost, including the expenditure to keep Barrow and Darfield Main in operation, would not be significantly lower than the preferred scheme and operating costs would be higher.

18. The choice of coal preparation plant represented a further subset of alternatives. Having regard to other projects taking place within the wider

Yorkshire Coking Coal Strategy, for example, at the central washery at Wooley servicing Barnsley Area's west side collieries, the Board asked the Area to appraise three alternative coal preparation plants:

(a) A fully flexible washery capable of servicing the same markets as now, but in varying proportions. These markets included metallurgical coking coal, Coalite semi-coking coal, CEGB, and washed graded coals for industry, domestic markets or export.

(b) As above except that there would be no provision for metallurgical coking coal and a special export graded coal would be lost. This scheme would not allow for increased sales into the industrial market but would allow existing industrial markets to be serviced.

(c) A basic plant which would essentially service the CEGB only. Other market commitments would be transferred to other pits, assuming this were possible.

19. The capital costs of these three types of central washing were estimated to be £51·8 million, £45·3 million and £40·3 million respectively. The Board also considered the possibility of investing a further £5·5 million on the fully flexible washery to provide re-wash facilities to meet a particular export order from Scandinavia for coal of a very demanding specification, but it rejected the proposal on the advice of Headquarters Marketing Department because of the high degree of risk associated with the estimate of prospective incremental revenue. On the advice of its Marketing Department, the Board elected to invest in a fully flexible washery (excluding the re-wash facility) in order to be able to attract and accommodate the planned expansion in the industrial market.

Financial appraisal

20. On the advice of the Marketing Department the Board paper included an alternative which revised downwards the Area's projected average proceeds of £35·45 per tonne (based on the carbonisation formula) to £33·13 per tonne (based on the lower industrial formula). The effect was to reduce the projected net present value of the total project (when discounted at 10 per cent) from £102 million to £62 million. Adopting the lower price assumption, the marginal DCF yield of the project when compared with the 'do nothing' alternative was calculated to be 20 per cent before risk. After allowing for the combined risk of: a one year's delay in completion, a 20 per cent increase in project costs, and a 10 per cent shortfall in both marginal proceeds and operating cost savings, the prospective marginal yield reduces to 11 per cent. The overall DCF yield of the colliery or complex was estimated to be 19 per cent before risk, or 7 per cent after risk rating.

21. A summary of Headquarters' view of the effects of the preferred project and the 'do nothing' alternative on output and operating margin for the individual collieries is shown below.

144

	A: 1978—79 Actual			B: Do nothing alternative (£91m)			1983—84 C: Preferred project (£112m)		
	Out-put '000t	Operating surplus/(loss) £'000	£/te	Out-put '000t	Operating surplus/(loss) £'000	£/te	Out-put '000t	Operating surplus/(loss) £'000	£/te
Grimethorpe	876	3,317	3·79	1,268	9,337	7·36	1,139	11,359	9·97
Houghton	662	(1,270)	(1·91)	1,398	10,887	7·79	1,295	13,225	10·21
Darfield	414	1,026	2·48	405	(103)	(0·25)	370	881	2·38
Barrow	334	(5,840)	(17·50)	645	(364)	(0·56)	564	1,126	2·00
Total	2,286	(2,765)	(1·21)	3,716	19,757	5·32	3,368	26,591	7·89
Interest at 11% pa and amortisation		3,124	1·37		17,887	4·84		21,062	6·25
Total net profit/(loss)		(5,889)	(2·58)		1,770	0·48		5,529	1·64

Conclusions and recommendations

22. The Mining Department advised that the benefits anticipated from the concentration of the four pits clearly justified the drivage of a straight drift rather than a zig-zag drift which would serve only Grimethorpe and Houghton Main lower levels; in addition it advised that the straight drift presented less mining engineering problems. The alternative arrangement, while enhancing the results of Grimethorpe and Houghton Main, was not considered attractive because the cost, combined with the necessary expenditure to maintain Barrow and Darfield Main in operation, would not be significantly lower than the preferred scheme and would not provide the reductions in operating costs forthcoming from the combine.

23. The main recommendation in the Mining Committee paper was that Barnsley Area be given Stage II approval in principle for the expenditure of £112·3 million at September 1979 prices, on the Grimethorpe South Side Project.

24. The Board granted approval at a meeting of the Mining Committee on 20 December 1979 and the Area was informed by the Board's Secretariat in January 1980.

Management of the project

25. The Annual Review of the project made in January 1982 reported that an additional nine months' slippage had occurred since the last Annual Review making a total of fifteen months' slippage. The revised completion date for the project was given as June 1984. The reason given for the additional slippage was restrictions on spending. The first full year of output was forecast to be 1985—86. Details of the latest estimates as given in the Annual Review of costs, output, productivity, etc relating to the project compared to the Stage II estimates and the estimate in the previous Annual Review are set out at Annex 1.

26. Under the overall control of the project manager (who for this project was of Chief Mining Engineer level) surface site management at Grimethorpe, including of the coal preparation plant, had been entrusted to a firm of consulting engineers. A firm of quantity surveyors was appointed to assist the project team. An organisational chart of the project team is at Annex 2.

27. The project manager maintained a bar chart of the whole project; the chart was updated at monthly intervals. The planned rates of drivages for future periods and actual drivages for past periods were shown on the bar chart. The planned drivages were updated at quarterly intervals. Actual progress was compared with planned progress for the quarter. The chart did not show cumulative progress to date against accumulative plans although a separate record is kept of this for drivages. Physical progress of surface work was indicated by shading in the bars.

28. A series of meetings took place weekly, fortnightly, monthly and quarterly to discuss and review various aspects of progress on the project. Details of these meetings are set out at Annex 3.

29. A number of reports were made at daily, weeky, monthly and quarterly intervals. Details of these various reports are at Annex 4.

30. Critical path charts were maintained by the consulting engineers on various aspects of the project. These were drawn up by hand. Some experiments with a computer package had been made but it had not proved satisfactory. Not all contractors on the project produced critical path charts. It was not a condition of their contracts. Detailed bar charts were maintained by contractors and by consultants to control progress.

Barnsley Area

Date of Approval 9 January 1980

Colliery scheme Grimethorpe—South Side project

Annual Review as at January 1982

	Revised Stage II estimate	Estimate in previous review	Latest estimate
1. Month and year of physical completion	March 1983	September 1983	June 1984
2. First full year of output after completion of the scheme	1983–84	1984–85	1985–86
3. Cost of scheme (£'000)			
(a) Capital	109,033	124,220	146,370
(b) Revenue	3,311	689	972
(c) Total cost	112,344	124,909	147,342
Expenditure to date (£'000)	—	6,062	24,928
Further expenditure committed (£'000)	—	40	51,023
4. Saleable output ('000 tonnes)	3,369	3,367·5	3,632·4
5. OMS/EMS ('000 tonnes/£)			
(a) Production	See next page	—	—
(b) Overall			
6. Manpower (overall face trained)			
(a) Total required	See next page		
(b) Numbers saved (where scheme provides)	See next page		
7. Workable reserves (m tonnes)	See next page		

Financial results

	Revised submission Stage II		Stage II at current price levels		Latest estimates	
	£'000	£/tonne	£'000	£/tonne	£'000	£/tonne
8. (a) Total investment (£'000)	186,774	55·46	226,855	67·37	259,033	71·31
(b) Profit—(loss) account						
(i) Proceeds	111,578·1	33·13	145,697	43·27	154,975	42·66
(ii) Operating costs	84,988·1	25·24	115,364	34·26	120,250	33·10
(iii) Profit/(loss) before interest	26,590·0	7·89	30,333	9·01	34,725	9·56
(iv) Interest and amortisation	20,975·3	6·23	25,978	7·72	30,564	8·41
(v) Profit/(loss) after interest	5,614·7	1·66	4,355	1·29	4,161	1·15
(c) Return on total investment	3·0%		1·9%		1·6%	

Colliery scheme Grimethorpe—South Side project

Annual review at January 1982

Date of approval 9 January 1980

		Stage II estimate revised	Differences in Manpower Oct 79 and completion	Scheme Savings Stage I plus Stage II	Estimate in previous review	Differences in Manpower Dec 80 and completion	Scheme Savings Stage I plus Stage II	Latest estimate	Differences in Manpower Dec 81 and completion	Scheme Savings Stage I plus Stage II
5. OMS/EMS (tonnes/£)										
Grimethorpe colliery										
(a) Production		16·24/–			16·24/–			17·44/–		
(b) Overall		3·49/–			8·49/–			3·88/–		
Barrow colliery										
(a) Production		8·53/–			8·53/–			11·34/–		
(b) Overall		2·54/–			2·54/–			2·76/–		
Darfield Main colliery										
(a) Production		9·28/–			9·28/–			7·56/–		
(b) Overall		2·63/–			2·63/–			2·35/–		
Houghton Main colliery										
(a) Production		13·86/–			13·86/–			11·82/–		
(b) Overall		4·17/–			4·17/–			3·52/–		
6. Manpower (overall face trained)										
Grimethorpe colliery										
(a) Total required	(+)	1729/437			1729/437			1733/488		
(b) Numbers saved required	(−)		–471	–208		–400	–208		–264	–208
Barrow colliery										
(a) Total required	(+)	1180/434			1180/434			1154/425		
(b) Numbers saved required	(−)		–337	–218		–269	–218		–215	–218
Darfield Main colliery										
(a) Total required	(+)	737/307			737/307			749/280		
(b) Numbers saved required	(−)		–123	–86		–83	–86		–24	–86
Houghton Main colliery										
(a) Total required	(+)	1584/479			1584/479			1573/544		
(b) Numbers saved required	(−)		–10	–10		–63	–10		–24	–18
New CPP at Grimethorpe										
(a) Total required	(+)	175/–			175/–			175/–		
(b) Numbers saved required	(−)		+175	+175		+175	+175		+175	+175
Total										
(a) Total required	(+)	5405/1657			5405/1657			5389/1737		
(b) Numbers saved required	(−)		–766	–355		–640	–355		–352	–355
7. Workable reserve (m tonnes)										
Grimethorpe colliery		61·3			61·6			58·8		
Barrow colliery		17·7			15·9			16·2		
Darfield Main colliery		9·1			8·1			8·3		
Houghton Main colliery		27·7			27·4			31·0		
Total		115·8			113·0			114·3		

ANNEX 2 TO APPENDIX 9.2(*b*)
(referred to in paragraph 26)

Organisation chart for the Grimethorpe projects team

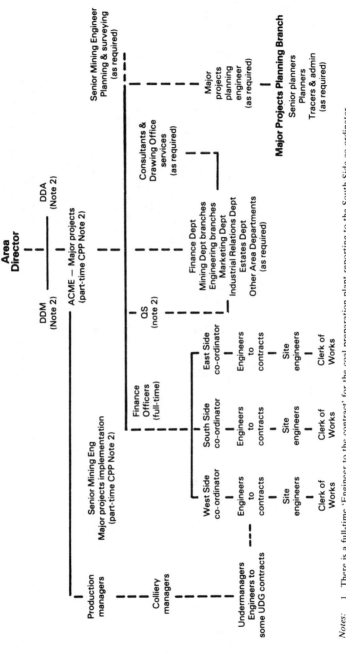

Notes: 1. There is a full-time 'Engineer to the contract' for the coal preparation plant reporting to the South Side co-ordinator.

2. Abbreviations used: DDM—Deputy Director Mining, CPP—Coal preparation plant, QS—Quantity Surveyor, UDG—Underground DDA—Deputy Director Admin, ACME—Area Chief Mining Eng (Major Projects)

149

Project meetings

Title	Objectives	Frequency	Membership
Weekly review meeting	Discussion of the activities which occurred during the week. Progress achieved. Problems which have arisen. Planning and co-ordinating.	Weekly	Engineer to the Project Representatives from —Coal preparation (Area) —Purchasing & Stores (Area) —Area electrical engineer —Safety engineer —Chartered quantity surveyors —Consulting engineers —Main contractor
Design meeting	To discuss all aspects of the engineering designs.	Weekly	Senior Eng (Reconstruction) Consulting Engineers Engineer to Projects Consulting quantity surveyors
Purchasing and contracts control meeting	Formal approval of tender list. Acceptance of tenders and to ensure competitive choice of purchases.	Weekly	Chief Mining Engineer (Major projects) Senior Mining Engineer (Major projects) Senior Engineer (Reconstruction) Chief Accountant Purchasing and Stores Department representative

Meeting	Purpose	Frequency	Attendees
Project meeting	To discuss the progress on all the projects in the Area.	Weekly/ Fortnightly	Chief Mining Eng (Major projects) Senior Mining Eng (Major projects in implementation) Co-ordinators Senior Eng (Reconstruction) Finance representatives Purchasing & Stores representative
Major projects meeting	To discuss expenditure against allocation, and the physical progress for the entire South Side project.	Monthly or every other month	Senior Mining Eng (Major projects implementation) Project co-ordinator The Engineers to the contracts Site Finance Officer Quantity Surveyors
Electrical meeting	To discuss specific aspects of the project which have an electrical content, eg Instrumentation Control.	Approximately monthly	Varies depending upon the topic under discussion —Electrical Engineer —Representatives from contractors —NCB Tech depts as required
Area executive meeting	As part of this meeting the overall progress and financial status of each project is discussed.	Monthly	Area Director Deputy Directors Area Chief Mining Eng (Major projects) Area Chief Mining Eng Area Chief Accountant Area Marketing Manager Area IR Officer Area Secretary
Major projects meeting	To discuss physical and financial progress against budget/allocation. (Review and accountability).	Quarterly	Chief Mining Engineer (Major projects) Senior Mining Engineer (Major projects) Senior Engineer (Reconstruction) Project Co-ordinators Quantity Surveyors Finance Department representative Planning Department representative Engineering Department representative

Reports

Source	Title	Contents	Audience
Admin Officer	Daily reports	Unusual occurrences and items that need to be highlighted and underground drivage progress.	Chief Mining Eng (major projects, Senior Mining Eng (major projects implementation) Co-ordinator, Senior Eng (reconstruction) and Engineer to Contract
Engineer to Contract	Minutes to the weekly site review meeting	Safety, progress, discussion of problems, planning co-ordination and contractual matters.	As above, plus: All technical depts, Coal Prep, Doncaster Contract branch of Purchasing and Stores (HQ), Major Projects Planners and MRD (Coal Prep Section)

Quantity Surveyors	Monthly progress report	Details of financial and physical progress of each project as a whole and in particular regard to contracts
		—Contract value
		—Variation orders
		—Contracts committed
		—Current position
		—Expected value of contract
		—Spending against allocation: monthly and cumulative
		—Spending against authorisation.
			Engineer to the Contract Circulated within:
			  Technical depts
			  Finance dept
			  Quantity Surveyor contracts representative

Finance Dept	Monthly capital report	Expenditure against allocation, monthly & accumulative. Actual against authorised expenditure; commitment against authorisation; authorisation compared with Stage II approval.	Area executives
Finance Dept	Fixed asset accounting (monthly)	Expenditure monthly, annual and cumulative by section compared with Stage II approval and Stage III authorisation. Committed and actual expenditure compared with authorisation.	Finance document available to others when required
Planning Branch of Mining Depts	Quarterly progress report	Actual expenditure against Stage II & III. Latest estimated cost. Percentage completion (Financial & Physical) Stage II completion date. Expected completion date.	Area Finance Dept HQ Mining Dept Area Mining Dept

Source	Title	Contents	Audience
Finance Dept	Latest estimated cost (quarterly)	Latest estimated cost of each project by sections with analyses of reasons for cost increases over Stage II approval ie price increases and other costs. Actual expenditure for the period and cumulative. Committed expenditure.	Area executive HQ Mining Dept Major Projects Planners
Finance Dept	Accountability statement (quarterly)	Forms basis of Area's accountability to Board. Includes Stage II cost, latest estimated cost, slippage since previous statement, actual expenditure this year to date, balance of expenditure for current year—total expenditure so far on project, total expenditure expected this year.	Area executives & Board
Finance Dept Tech Depts	Annual Review	On the anniversary date of the Stage II, approval on annual review is presented to HQ. The review is a compact updating of the Stage III.	Project Review Committee

Oakdale

Nature and main objectives of the project

1. The proposal put forward by the South Wales Area was to access a new area of reserves to the south of Oakdale and Celynen North collieries containing some 9·8 million tonnes of prime coking coals. The scheme included the provision of new fast man-riding materials haulage facilities and mineral conveyors to serve the new area. The objective of the project was to extend the life of the Oakdale Combine by some 10 years and avoid a reduction in output from 1984–85 onwards.

Background to the project

2. In October 1975 the Board approved a scheme to connect underground Oakdale, Markham and Celynen North collieries, with the combined output of these collieries being brought to the surface of Oakdale; the Oakdale coal preparation plant was to be expanded and improved to handle the increased output arriving there. The development of the southern reserves was envisaged at the time of the reorganisation scheme and £1·6 million at April 1975 price levels (£2·8 million at May 1979 price levels) was included in the colliery cash flows.

3. The reorganisation scheme was planned to be completed by March 1979 with a projected annual saleable output of 902,000 tonnes (at an OMS of 2·16 tonnes) and manpower savings of 273. However, operational difficulties had delayed the project and the Area expected the first full year of production to be 1980–81 and annual saleable output 800,000 tonnes.

Stage I

4. The Area had not submitted a Stage I proposal to Headquarters concerning the southern reserves because the project had already been discussed in the context of the reorganisation scheme which had obtained Stage II approval.

Stage II

5. The Board paper provided a summary of the financial history of the three collieries forming the Oakdale Combine. The figures are summarised in the table below:

Oakdale colliery (including Markham and Celynen North tables of results)

Oakdale

Year	Saleable output ('000 tonnes)	OMS (tonnes)		Operating surplus/ (loss)		Average manpower
		Face	Overall	£'000	£ per tonne	
1974–75	413	5·95	1·91	1,509	3·65	1,025
1975–76	391	5·39	1·80	2,806	7·17	1,061
1976–77	419	5·92	1·98	4,093	9·79	1,066
1977–78	333	4·93	1·59	1,697	5·09	1,050
1978–79	320	4·69	1·59	819	2·56	997
1979–80 1st quarter	33	3·67	0·86	(1,397)	(42·51)	965

Markham

1974–75	209	5·63	1·85	277	1·32	572
1975–76	237	5·81	1·94	1,160	4·90	626
1976–77	233	5·75	1·89	1,548	6·65	638
1977–78	234	5·25	1·85	1,642	7·01	647
1978–79	216	5·57	1·72	898	4·17	629
1979–80 1st quarter	48	6·06	1·61	52	1·08	626

Celynen North

1974–75	156	3·14	1·02	(998)	(6·36)	765
1975–76	174	3·34	1·16	(777)	(4·47)	786
1976–77	134	2·79	0·89	(1,928)	(14·38)	800
1977–78	143	3·19	0·95	(1,904)	(13·29)	767
1978–79	183	5·57	1·30	(934)	(5·11)	713
1979–80 1st quarter	40	4·77	1·23	(422)	(10·69)	669

Source: The NCB.

6. The Area estimated that without the project the reserves available to the three collieries forming the combine amounted to 12·8 million tonnes, sufficient for 18 years' life at the planned rate of production. The benefits of accessing the southern reserves lay not only in prolonging the life of the combine by 10 years but also in facilitating the policy of carefully phased working to avoid interaction and over-concentration by working faces in both the northern and southern areas simultaneously.

7. *Alternatives.* The Area and Headquarters Mining Department considered the possibility of delaying entry into the southern area reserves and concentrating activity in the northern reserves. However, the Mining Department's view was that the mine would suffer from a lack of flexibility, geological interruptions and increased interaction difficulties; it considered therefore that it would become more difficult for the mine to achieve the forecast output levels. The Mining Department therefore supported the principle of making an early entry into the southern reserves.

8. The submission also presented an alternative to the means of accessing the new area envisaged in the reorganisation scheme. The Area considered that the roadway planned in, and part of, the reorganisation scheme had deteriorated to the extent that it would be quicker and less expensive to drive a new roadway.

9. *Cost of the project.* The cost of the project at May 1979 price levels based on technical estimates by NCB engineers was forecast to be £7,767,884 of which £581,091 was allocated to revenue account; the estimate excluded plant pool items costing £137,836. The Board paper summarised the main details of the proposal and their estimated cost as follows:

	£'000
General expenses including the disposal of dirt from drivages via Celynen North shafts	603
Drivage equipment, conveyors, bunker and haulage equipment including also the installation of pumps, fans and methane drainage equipment complete with associated electrics	1,613
The drivage of access roads (210 metres), crosscuts conveyor roads (390 metres), new face line, booster fan sites and pump and haulage houses	1,420
The drivage of the intake roadway (1,660 metres) from the inbye end of the Celynen North conveyor connection at 18 metres/week	1,524
The drivage of the return roadway (2,915 metres) to be driven simultaneously in two directions from a new access road from Celynen North belt conveyor road (into the southern reserves and north to connect with the Oakdale pitbottom loco road) at 18 metres/week in each direction	2,736
	7,916
Less credit for coal from drivages	149
(excluding plant pool costs of £137,836)	7,767

10. *Marketing.* The views of Headquarters Marketing Department were contained in the Board paper. The department supported the project because, provided the quality of coal was maintained as forecast, the comparatively low production costs made the project an attractive investment. It considered that the production of low/medium volatile Welsh coking coals would, with this scheme and the new mine at Margam, broadly equate with the British Steel Corporation's overall demand in the late 1980s. This, it said, afforded the opportunity to displace some or all of the imports (about 750,000 tonnes per annum) which were augmenting local supplies.

11. *The Mining Department's views.* The Mining Department supported the project but considered that, in view of operational difficulties being experienced in the reorganisation scheme, the lack of detailed knowledge of the geological conditions, and the fact that face conditions might be poorer in the southern reserves, the Area's forecast of 902,000 tonnes saleable output per annum could well prove optimistic. Although the Area

156

was asked to aim for the forecast output, lower output forecasts were agreed as follows:

	With project	Without project
	'000 tonnes	'000 tonnes
1979–80	700	700
1980–81 to 1983–84	800	800
1984–85 onwards	850	700

12. *The Finance Department's views.* Headquarters Finance Department estimated that on the basis of the Mining Department's output projections the net profit (ie after interest charges) in the year after completion (at July 1979 price levels) would be £5·9 million compared with £2·7 million in the 'no project' situation. Adopting the same output assumptions for its DCF appraisal, the Finance Department estimated a net present value for the colliery cash flow with the project of £78·8 million (with the cash flows discounted at 10 per cent per annum over 20 years) and a corresponding figure of £58·7 million without the project; the marginal DCF yield of the project was estimated to be 32 per cent.

13. In the Board paper the Finance Department stated that the colliery cash flows with the project were sufficiently robust to withstand the combined risks of a 20 per cent reduction in output/proceeds (ie output reducing to 680,000 tonnes per annum), a two-year delay in project completion and a 20 per cent increase in project costs and still give a positive NPV when discounted at 10 per cent. After the same marginal risks, the marginal cash flow would still provide a 10 per cent DCF yield. It was estimated that 'if output were the only risk a 40 per cent reduction in marginal output would be covered'.

14. The Board paper also provided estimates of the colliery NPV and the marginal yield of the project according to the Area's original estimate of annual output.

Stage II approval
15. The Mining Committee considered the proposal on 13 September 1979 and gave Stage II approval to the project; the Area was formally notified on 3 October 1979. In agreeing the proposal the Board requested the Area to achieve an annual output from the combine of 0·9 million tonnes.

Management of the project
16. The first Annual Review of the project made in October 1980 reported that the project was expected to be completed on time, ie by February 1983. However, since the Stage II submission the market situation had changed with the slump in the steel industry with a consequent substantial reduction in demand for coking coals, especially the lower volatile coals such as Oakdale washed smalls. The market emphasis had changed with over 70 per cent of washed smalls shown as going to power stations. The reduction in proceeds because of the lower price per tonne together with a forecast increase in operating costs of 30 per cent since the Stage II

157

submission meant that Stage II estimate of operating surplus of £8·5 million (£4·4 million at updated price levels) was replaced by a forecast of an operating loss of £1·1 million.

17. At the time of the second Annual Review in December 1981 the completion of the project had slipped by approximately nine months and it was now forecast to be completed by December 1983. There had been another change in the market emphasis over the period and disposals of Oakdale washed smalls had swung back to the coke oven market. However, because the price of coking coals had not risen in line with cost inflation, proceeds had fallen in real terms and the operating loss in the first full year of operation (1984–85) was forecast to be £3·2 million. Details of the latest estimates as given in the Annual Review of cost, output, productivity etc relating to the project compared to the Stage II estimates and the estimates in the previous Annual Review are set at Annex 1.

18. The project manager was the Production Manager for the collieries who was engaged on the project part-time. An organisational chart of the project team is at Annex 2.

19. Bar charts were used to plan and control progress but no critical path networks were maintained.

20. A series of meetings were held weekly, monthly and quarterly to discuss and review various aspects of progress on the project. Details of these meetings are set out at Annex 3.

21. A number of reports were made at daily, weekly, monthly, quarterly and annual intervals. Details of these reports are set out at Annex 4.

ANNEX 1 TO APPENDIX 9.2(c)
(referred to in paragraph 17)

South Wales Area
Oakdale colliery

Annual Review as at 26 December 1981
Development of southern reserves

		Stage II estimate Feb 1983 1983–84	Estimate in previous review Feb 1983 1983–84	Latest estimate Dec 1983 1984–85
Month and year of physical completion		Feb 1983	Feb 1983	Dec 1983
First full year of output after completion of the scheme		1983–84	1983–84	1984–85
Cost of scheme	(£'000)			
(a) Capital		7,187	8,625	10,319
(b) Revenue		581	728	230
(c) Total cost		7,768	9,353	10,549
Expenditure to date	(£'000)	—	842	4,082
Further expenditure committed	(£'000)	—	1,246	954
Saleable output	('000 tonnes)	902	1,054	850
OMS/EMS	('000 tonnes/£)			
(a) Production		6·45/£23·99	7·53/£28·33	7·84/£29·19
(b) Overall		2·19/£21·62	2·56/£25·64	2·00/£28·39
Manpower (overall/face trained)		2,068	2,068	2,040/830
Workable reserves (million tonnes)		23·2	19·6	23·3

Financial results

	Original submission Stage II		Stage II at current price levels		Latest estimate	
	£'000	£/tonne	£'000	£/tonne	£'000	£/tonne
(a) Total investment	32,033	35·52	41,720	46·25	80,444	94·64
(b) Profit—(loss) account						
(i) Proceeds	37,706	41·82	41,479	46·00	38,358	45·13
(ii) Operating costs	29,161	32·34	39,377	43·66	41,573	48·91
(iii) Profit/(Loss) before interest	8,545	9·48	2,102	2·34	(3,215)	(3·78)
(iv) Interest and amortisation	3,636	4·03	4,721	5·24	8,967	10·55
(v) Profit/(Loss) after interest	4,909	5·45	(2,619)	(2·90)	(12,182)	(14·33)
(c) Return on total investment	15·3%					

159

Organisation chart of the project team

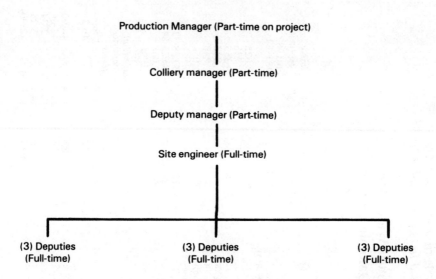

Production Manager (Part-time on project)

Colliery manager (Part-time)

Deputy manager (Part-time)

Site engineer (Full-time)

| (3) Deputies | (3) Deputies | (3) Deputies |
| (Full-time) | (Full-time) | (Full-time) |

Plus: Project Cost Control officer
(Part-time)

Project planner
(Part-time)

Project meetings

Title	Purpose	Membership
Weekly progress meeting	Progress and payments to contractors' future plans	Colliery manager, operational planner, cost control officer, site engineer, surveyor, contractors' representatives.
Monthly progress meeting	Progress achieved. Appraisal of financial position	Production manager, representative from purchasing and stores, project planner, colliery managers, contracts officer, senior planning engineer, site engineer, project planning engineer, project cost control officer, progress section surveyor.
Monthly payment meeting	Progress and payments to contractors	As monthly progress meeting plus contractors' representatives.
Monthly accountability meeting	Colliery accountability	Production manager, colliery manager.
Quarterly planning meeting	Colliery accountability (project will be discussed in the context of the colliery)	Area chief mining engineer, deputy Area chief mining engineer, production manager, Area planning engineer, Area method study engineer, senior planner, colliery manager, colliery surveyors.
Area accountability meeting	As appropriate	Area director, deputy director mining, chief mining engineer.
Accountability meeting with HQ	Quarterly	At director level.

Reports

Title	Contents	Frequency	Audience
Shift report book	Diary of events during shift	Every shift	Site engineer, colliery manager.
Site engineer diary	Diary of events measure of work done	Daily shift by shift	Cost control office, general manager, progressing documents.
Weekly work summary	Accumulation of work done and payments to contractors	Weekly	Colliery management, Area management, project team contractor, purchasing and stores representative.
Monthly progress meetings (minutes of)	Review of finance and physical progress develop future action plan	Monthly	Project team, Area management.
Monthly contractors' meeting (minutes of)	To discuss progress and payment	Monthly	Project team, Area management, contractors.
Expenditure report	Expenditure compared with Stage II & III	Monthly	Project team, Area management.
Quarterly progress report to HQ	Comparison of expenditure and progress against Stage II	Three-monthly	HQ Mining Department.
Annual Review	Comparison of expenditure and progress against Stage II with estimate of outcome	Annually	Project/Review Committees (HQ): with reference to accountability meeting between Area and Board members and Mining Committee if appropriate.
Final completion report	Review of actual expenditure in comparison with Stage II. Analysis and explanation of variations. Report on financial outturn compared with Stage II plus an explanation of variations.	One year after the completion of the project.	Project/Review Committees with paper to Mining Committee.

Estimated and actual output of the 77 completed projects

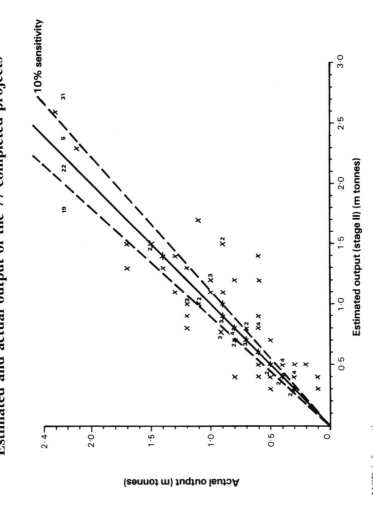

Source: MMC from NCB information.

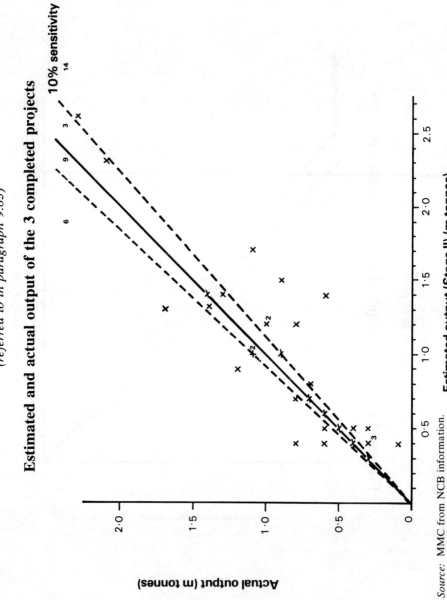

Estimated and actual output of the 3 completed projects

Source: MMC from NCB information.

Estimated and actual OMS of the 77 completed projects

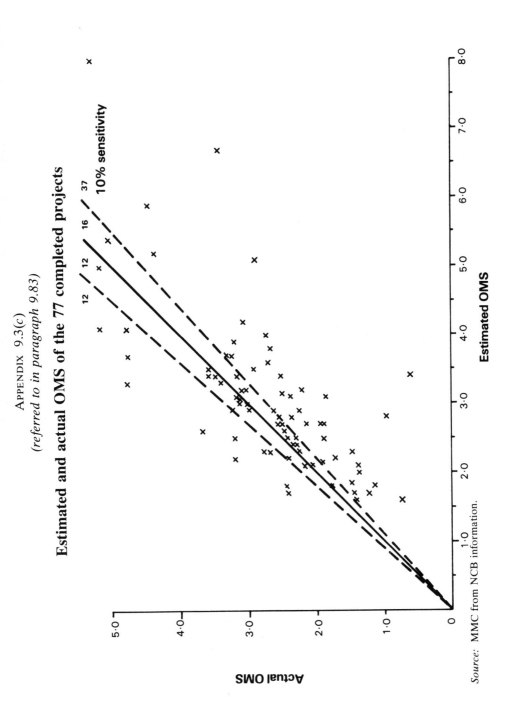

Source: MMC from NCB information.

165

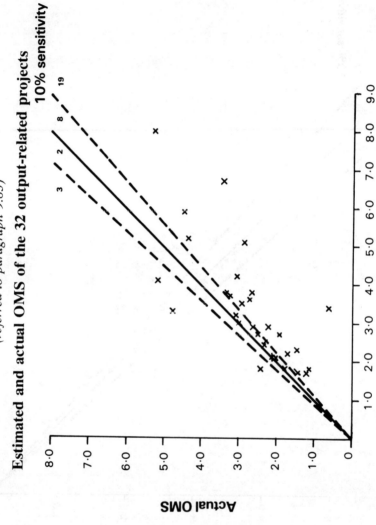

Estimated and actual OMS of the 32 output-related projects

10% sensitivity

Actual OMS

Estimated stage II OMS

Source: MMC from NCB information.

Estimated and actual completion times of the 77 completed projects

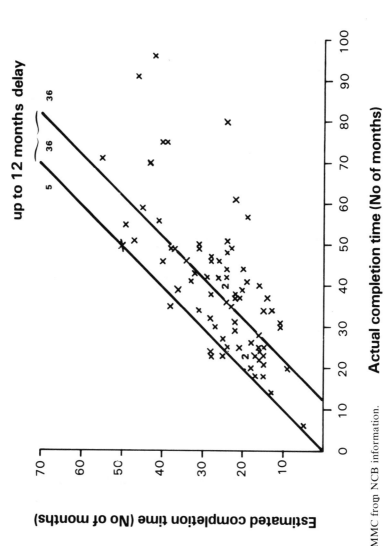

Source: MMC from NCB information.

Estimated and actual completion time of the 32 output-related projects

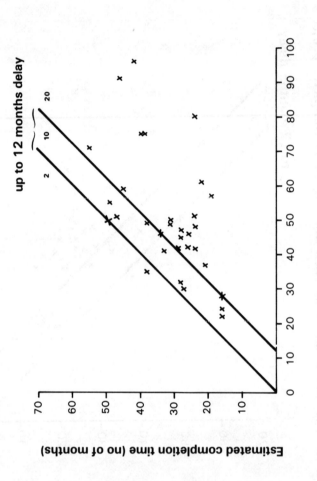

up to **12 months** delay

Estimated completion time (no of months)

Actual completion time (no of months)

Source: MMC frm NCB information.

Estimated and actual cost of the 77 completed projects

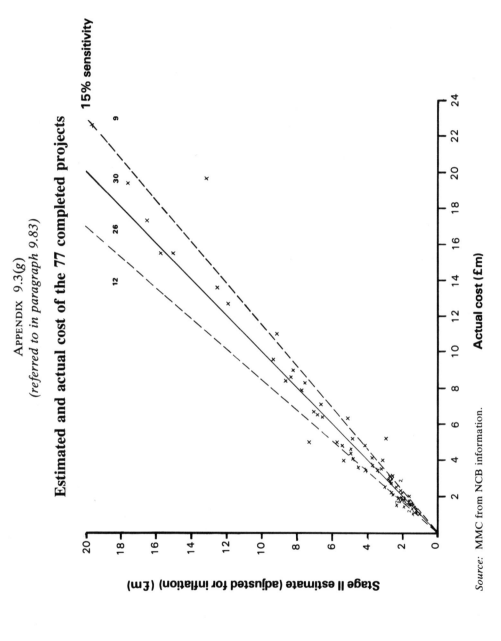

Source: MMC from NCB information.

APPENDIX 9.3(*h*)
(*referred to in paragraph 9.83*)

Estimated and actual cost of the 32 output-related projects

Source: MMC from NCB information.

Comparison between Stage II operating margins updated to 1981–82 costs
and proceeds, and operating margins achieved in 1981–82

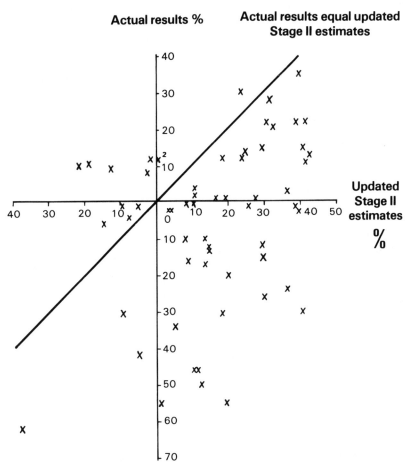

Actual results %

Actual results equal updated Stage II estimates

Updated Stage II estimates %

Notes:

(1) Four collieries' results lie beyond the range of this graph: three were below the 45° line and below minus 70; one was above the 45° line and beyond minus 40.

(2) No costs of production figures were available for four other collieries.

(3) No rapid loading projects were included in the analysis.

Source: MMC from NCB information.

Holditch

Objectives of the project

1. The objectives of the Holditch project were:

   (*a*) To replace the existing steam winders (which had been installed in 1918) in both shafts with second-hand electric winders transferred from another colliery. This was in line with national policy to replace all steam winding equipment at long life collieries with electric winders. It was estimated that the replacement would effect a saving of eight men per day and power, heat and light costs of £132,000 a year and £43,000 on reduced maintenance.

   (*b*) To install skip winding facilities in number 2 shaft thereby increasing the winding capacity to permit an increase in output to 559,000 tonnes a year.

   (*c*) To provide access to the deeper reserves of the colliery and thus extend the life of the colliery which would otherwise exhaust its reserves in 1985–86.

Background

2. Holditch is situated in the Western Area close to Newcastle-under-Lyme. At the time of the Stage II submission in December 1977 the colliery was producing around 370,000 tonnes of coal a year. The financial results of the colliery for 1976–77 showed an operating profit of £3·5 million (£9·23 per tonne); output per man-shift (OMS) was 2·79 tonnes. These figures compared with those for the Area of an operating loss of £21 million from an output of 11·3 million tonnes and an OMS of 2·2 tonnes.

Estimated results

3. The total cost of the project was estimated to be £4·7 million of which £3·8 million was capital expenditure and £0·9 million was revenue expenditure. The first full year of output was estimated in the Stage II submission to be 1981–82 although full benefits from the project would not be obtained until 1982–83, after the commissioning of the number 1 winder in July 1981.

4. The Stage II submission included estimates that in 1982–83 revenue would be £17·4 million and net profit after interest would be £6·5 million (£11·58 per tonne). OMS was forecast to increase by 42 per cent from 2·79 tonnes to 3·97 tonnes.

5. The undiscounted cash flows of the colliery with the project over 16 years were estimated to be £114·7 million which when discounted at 10 per cent gave a net present value of £57 million. The internal rate of return for the colliery with the project was in excess of 100 per cent.

Actual performance

6. The project was given Stage II approval in March 1978. Almost immediately the colliery ran into severe geological difficulties when it encountered a very extensive washout which resulted in a serious loss of output. In order to restore the lost output the colliery manager had to divert men from the project onto underground development in order to find reserves at the existing level. This led to a delay in the completion of the project and, although the principal objectives of the project (ie electrification of winder and installation of skips) were achieved by July 1981, the net effect is that the deeper seams are not expected to be accessed until March 1983, two years later than originally planned. In March 1982 the latest estimate of the total cost of the project was £7·0 million of which £6·3 million was capital expenditure and £0·7 million was revenue expenditure.

Management of the project

7. The project manager was the Western Area Senior Mining Engineer (Projects) who was engaged on the project part-time. An organisational chart of the project team is at Annex 1.

8. Bar charts were used to plan and control progress but no critical path networks were maintained.

9. A series of meetings were held weekly, fortnightly, monthly and quarterly to discuss and review various aspects of progress on the project. Details of these meetings are set out at Annex 2.

10. A number of reports were made at daily, weekly, monthly and quarterly intervals. Details of these various reports are at Annex 3.

Organisational chart

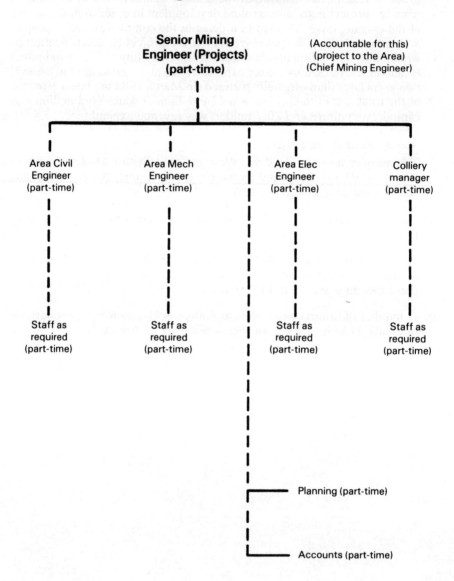

Project meetings

Title	Objectives	Frequency	Membership
Weekly pit meeting	Progress meeting to discuss the activities in the pit. Every second week the scope is enlarged and becomes the 'Production Control Meeting' which includes progressing of project drivages	Weekly	Colliery manager, deputy manager, unit mech. engineer, unit elec. engineer.
Production control meeting	Similar to the weekly pit meeting but covers an enlarged scope including project mining progress	Every two weeks	As above plus: store-keeper, heads of depts., deputy manager, deputy engineers.
Project progress meetings	For each section of the project there are separate progress meetings chaired by the relevant Area Eng.	Monthly per section	Appropriate Area, deputy Area, operations and unit engineers.
Project co-ordinating meeting	A co-ordinating meeting is held to monitor the progress achieved on the individual sections, chaired by the Senior Mining Engineer (Projects)	Every one to three months	Senior Mining Engineer, colliery engineers, operations engineer, planning, special projects engineer, admin. officer, production manager, colliery manager and senior finance officers.
Business planning meeting	As part of this meeting the overall progress and financial status of each project is discussed	Monthly	Area Director, Dep. Director Mining, Dep. Director Admin., Chief Mining Engineer, Dep. Chief Mining Eng., Area P & S Manager, Area I R Officer, Area planning engineer, Area Secretary, Area Marketing Manager, Area Chief Accountant, Area Chief Engineer.

Reports

Source	Title	Contents	Audience
Deputies	Shift work	Measurement of work done	Colliery under manager
Surveyor	Weekly report	Measurement of work done. Check on level and line	Colliery deputy manager
Colliery under manager	Weekly report	Accumulation of all the shift work sheets	Colliery deputy manager and manager
Planning department	Progress report updated monthly	Physical progress report, including bar charts updated monthly	Available to those who need to refer to it and submitted to HQ annually
Senior Mining Engineer (Projects)	Monthly report to the business planning team	Brief details of progress. Estimate of final cost. Amount spent to date	Business planning team
Accounts	Monthly financial report	Details of the financial expenditure against allocation	Area management
Area Planning Department & Accounts	Quarterly progress report	Brief progress reports concentrating on financial aspects but in addition including a simple bar chart of physical progress achieved	Area management & Headquarters Mining Department
Area Planning Department	Annual Review	On the anniversary date of the Stage II approval an annual review is presented to H.Q. The review is a compact updating of the Stage II and identifies the likely outcome of all facets	H.Q. Review Committee, Project Committee with paper to Mining Committee if appropriate

Organisation chart for the Selby project team

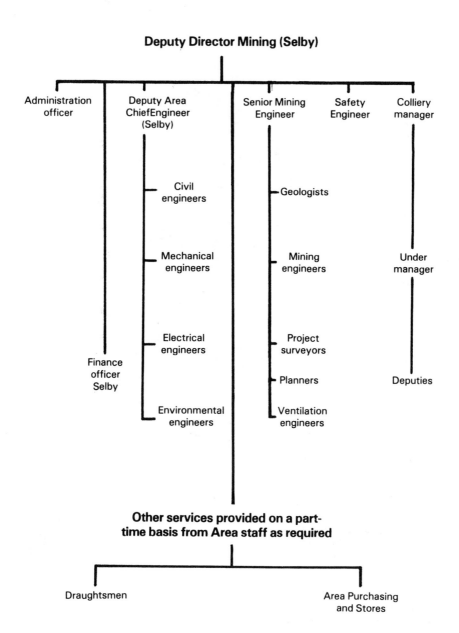

Deputy Director Mining (Selby)

Administration officer

Deputy Area ChiefEngineer (Selby)

Senior Mining Engineer

Safety Engineer

Colliery manager

Civil engineers

Geologists

Mechanical engineers

Mining engineers

Under manager

Electrical engineers

Project surveyors

Finance officer Selby

Planners

Deputies

Environmental engineers

Ventilation engineers

Other services provided on a part-time basis from Area staff as required

Draughtsmen

Area Purchasing and Stores

(referred to in paragraph 10.72)

The Selby new mine project original development plan
Underground physical progress (as at end September, 1981)

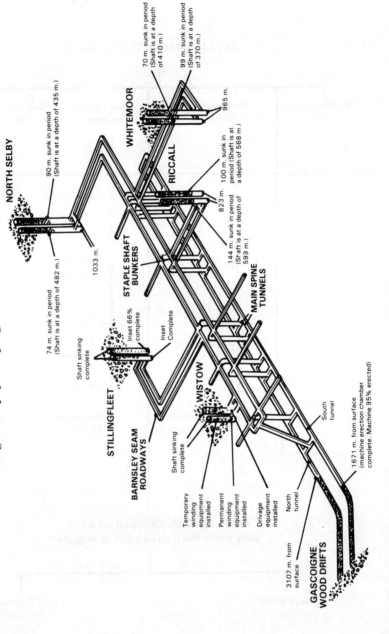

(referred to in paragraph 10.72)

The Selby new mine project revised development plan
Underground physical progress (as at end March, 1982)

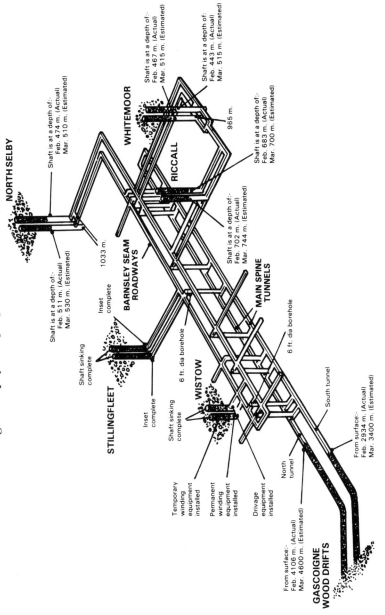

NORTH SELBY

WHITEMOOR

RICCALL

STILLINGFLEET

WISTOW

BARNSLEY SEAM ROADWAYS

MAIN SPINE TUNNELS

GASCOIGNE WOOD DRIFTS

Shaft is at a depth of:-
Feb. 474 m. (Actual)
Mar. 510 m. (Estimated)

Shaft is at a depth of:-
Feb. 467 m. (Actual)
Mar. 515 m. (Estimated)

Shaft is at a depth of:-
Feb. 443 m. (Actual)
Mar. 515 m. (Estimated)

Shaft is at a depth of:-
Feb. 683 m. (Actual)
Mar. 700 m. (Estimated)

Shaft is at a depth of:-
Feb. 702 m. (Actual)
Mar. 744 m. (Estimated)

Shaft is at a depth of:-
Feb. 511 m. (Actual)
Mar. 530 m. (Estimated)

965 m.

1033 m.

Inset complete

Shaft sinking complete

Inset complete

Shaft sinking complete

6 ft. dia borehole

6 ft. dia borehole

South tunnel

North tunnel

Temporary winding equipment installed

Permanent winding equipment installed

Drivage equipment installed

From surface:-
Feb. 2934 m. (Actual)
Mar. 3400 m. (Estimated)

From surface:-
Feb. 4106 m. (Actual)
Mar. 4600 m. (Estimated)

179

(referred to in paragraph 11.5)

NCB Opencast Executive saleable output 1952 to 1981–82 (on a 52-week year basis) (million tonnes)

1952	9·5
1953	11·7
1954	10·3
1955	11·5
1956	12·0
1957	13·3
1958	14·0
1959	10·7
1960	7·5
1961	8·6
1962	7·3
1963–64	7·0
1964–65	6·5
1965–66	6·9
1966–67	6·8
1967–68	7·0
1968–69	6·4
1969–70	6·3
1970–71	8·1
1971–72	10·1
1972–73	10·3
1973–74	9·0
1974–75	9·3
1975–76	10·4
1976–77	11·4
1977–78	13·6
1978–79	13·5
1979–80	13·0
1980–81	15·3
1981–82	14·3

Source: The NCB.

Opencast Regions

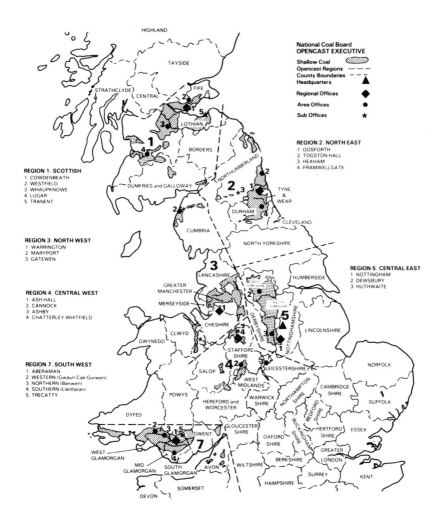

Source: The NCB.

(referred to in paragraphs 11.12 and 11.13)

The Opencast Executive
Non-industrial staff—salaries and related expenses

(a) Approximate annual costs at 30 April 1982, calculated by the application to staff numbers of multipliers suggested by the Opencast Executive as indicators of the average for the grades.

Region	Management		Clerical		Total		1981–82 Saleable output	Operating profit
	No of staff	Cost £'000	No of staff	Cost £'000	No of staff	Cost £'000	m tonnes	£m
Scottish	131	1,851·0	67	448·9	198	2,299·9	3·025	34·7
North East	127	1,795·0	63	422·1	190	2,217·1	3·076	31·0
North West	80	1,137·0	35	234·5	115	1,371·5	1·285	9·7
Central West	99	1,403·0	63	422·1	162	1,825·1	1·744	23·6
Central East	136	1,921·0	91	609·7	227	2,530·7	2·966	34·7
South West	131	1,851·0	110	737·0	241	2,588·0	2·253	23·2
	704	9,958·0	429	2,874·3	1,133	12,832·3	14·349	156·9
Headquarters	73	1,175·0	69	462·3	142	1,637·3	—	—
	777	11,133·0	498	3,336·6	1,275	14,469·6	14·349	156·9

Source: MMC from NCB information.

(b) £ per tonne of saleable output

	Tonnes '000 per person	Management £/te	Tonnes '000 per person	Clerical £/te	Tonnes '000 per person	Total £/te
Scottish	23·1	0·61	45·1	0·15	15·3	0·76
North East	24·2	0·58	48·8	0·14	16·2	0·72
North West	16·1	0·88	36·7	0·18	11·2	1·06
Central West	17·6	0·80	27·7	0·24	10·8	1·04
Central East	21·8	0·65	32·6	0·20	13·1	0·85
South West	17·2	0·82	20·5	0·33	9·3	1·15
Total including Headquarters	18·5	0·78	28·8	0·23	11·3	1·01

Source: MMC from NCB information.

(c) Staff numbers

Region	Management No	%	Clerical No	%	Total
Scottish	131	66·2	67	33·8	198
North East	127	66·8	63	33·2	190
North West	80	69·6	35	30·4	115
Central West	99	61·1	63	38·9	162
Central East	136	59·9	91	40·1	227
South West	131	54·4	110	45·6	241
Total including Headquarters	777	60·9	498	39·1	1,275

Source: MMC from NCB information.

(referred to in paragraph 11.54)

Note on incidence of and payment for excess coal in opencast sites

1. The incidence of excess coal varies considerably across the Regions. The following table (taken from a report by the Midlands Audit Centre—NCB Audit Department, October 1981) reviews the incidence of excess coal arising on 53 sites which have ceased coaling in the last three years or are still coaling.

Table 1 **Incidence of excess coal arising on sites which have ceased coaling in the last three years or which are still coaling**

Region	No of sites	Contract tonnage	Excess coal tonnage	Excess coal as% of contract tonnage
Scottish	8	6,236,675	139,358	2·2
North East	8	5,149,860	489,330	9·5
North West	3	400,780	18,028	4·5
Central West	4	740,419	112,059	15·1
Central East	17	8,818,619	1,197,752	13·6
South Western	13	7,433,534	1,673,251	22·5
Total	53	28,779,887	3,629,778	12·6

Source: Report by Midlands Audit Centre—NCB Audit Dept, October 1981.

To put this matter into perspective, over the same period shortfalls against contract tonnage occurred at seven sites throughout the Regions, amounting to on average 13 per cent of a total contract tonnage of 10·75 million tonnes. Shortfalls against contract tonnage would normally attract claims against the Executive.

2. It will be appreciated that the estimation of a contract tonnage by exploratory boring and extrapolation of the results cannot be expected to produce a figure of complete accuracy. The fact that shortfalls will give rise to claims without benefit of production can be expected to incline the Executive towards the lower end of the range of a site's potential tonnage for contract purposes. It will be seen from Table 1, however, that the ratio of excess coal to contract tonnage was highest in South-Western Region, being at 22·5 per cent nearly double the national average including South-Western Region of 12·6 per cent. Geological factors account for the wide range of variance between Regions with South-Western being particularly difficult. It has been the practice in this Region to allow generous tolerances from in-situ coal to provide partly for the problems of estimation and partly for the difficulties of coal recovery.

3. The audit report referred to above was particularly concerned with negotiations for payment for excess coal at three sites in South-Western Region, where excess coal was estimated to total 1·013 million tonnes against the combined contract tonnage of 2·331 million tonnes, giving excess coal at 43·46 per cent of contract tonnage overall. The figure for one particular site was 60·4 per cent. For this site, the ROD submitted to Executive

headquarters detailed proposals for establishing a rate for the excess coal which departed from the general rule of face rate less subsidiary items and attempted to relate the price to the contractors' additional work and costs. A separate calculation was made at Executive headquarters, based upon the downward change in the rates of overburden to coal, and the resulting amended face rate was given to the ROD as a negotiating limit. The rate finally negotiated was within this limit. For the second site the basis of settlement was related to the Executive headquarters formula for the first one. Both these sites were let by single tender negotiation, to which reference is made in paragraph 11·55. The rate for the excess coal at the third site, let by competitive tender, was established close to the contract face rate less subsidiaries. The NCB Audit Department considered that because of the extent of excess coal compared to contract coal, and on the basis of the principles adopted in the ROD's proposed method for the first site, there was a strong case for negotiating a price lower than contract face rate less subsidiaries for excess coal on the second site, and on the third site. However, the Executive pointed out to Audit Department that the calculations were different ways of assessing a future operation for which the contract price was incapable of precise evaluation. Both evaluations, and indeed others presented by the contractor himself, needed to be taken in account when the rate was finally negotiated.

(referred to in paragraphs 11.60 and 11.61)

Opencast Executive—profit and loss accounts before NCB Headquarters adjustments

	Year to end of March					
	1977	*1978*	*1979*	*1980*	*1981*	*1982*
Tonnes '000						
Saleable	11,431	13,551	13,801	13,013	15,279	14,349
Disposals	11,770	13,028	12,701	13,730	12,472	14,593
Stock change	−339	523	1,100	−717	2,807	−244
Stock at end	1,069	1,592	2,692	1,975	4,782	4,538
Proceeds £'000						
Disposals	235,719	298,803	321,882	412,842	435,649	550,493
Stock change	−7,223	13,812	34,051	−23,513	97,841	−10,494
Saleable	228,496	312,615	355,933	389,329	533,490	539,999
Market rebates	−7,021	−7,126	−10,011	−14,224		
Stocking provision	4,537	−1,528	−4,718	14,317	−9,435	18,531
Sundry sales and service charges	490	678	1,000	541	1,174	1,830
Net proceeds	226,502	304,639	342,204	389,963	525,229	560,360
Costs						
Production contractual	119,981	164,262	187,600	207,045	268,423	281,043
Haulage to disposal point	5,299	7,226	8,028	8,995	13,481	14,497
Preparation contractual	9,920	12,451	13,339	17,844	19,158	25,163
Other site and DP expenses	2,653	5,308	8,188	8,492	9,471	13,408
Depreciation	6,853	1,507	2,145	2,461	3,257	3,462
Rehabilitation and compensation	8,047	7,942	8,256	10,891	15,036	17,255
Sub-total	152,753	198,696	227,556	255,728	328,826	354,828
Major revenue expenditure	1,104	1,507	1,537	1,969	2,991	3,247
Prospecting and boring	3,432	4,459	5,692	8,265	11,253	11,991
Gross social costs	63	34	154	76	993	
OE overheads and services	9,411	11,526	12,975	15,118	19,269	20,418
Headquarters overheads and services	1,700	1,950	2,750	3,300	3,900	4,300
Total costs	168,463	218,172	250,664	284,456	367,232	394,784
Operating profit	58,039	86,467	91,540	105,507	157,997	165,576
£ per tonne						
Net proceeds per tonne saleable	19·81	22·48	24·79	29·97	34·38	39·05
Total costs per tonne saleable	14·74	16·09	18·16	21·86	24·04	27·51
Operating profit per tonne saleable	5·07	6·39	6·63	8·11	10·34	11·54
	%	%	%	%	%	%
Ratios						
Total costs as % of net proceeds	74·37	71·62	73·25	72·94	69·92	70·45
Operating profit as % of net proceeds	25·63	28·38	26·75	27·06	30·08	29·55

Source: MMC from NCB information.

The Executive's costs are related to headings in the Opencast Executive's profit and loss accounts as follows:

(i) The cost of acquiring working rights, leases and compensation payments are debited to the headings Rehabilitation and Compensation over the working life of the site.

(ii) Proving of workable reserves: the actual costs incurred during the year are charged to the heading 'Prospecting and boring'.

(iii) All amounts payable to coaling site contractors under their contracts, including the Restoration Lump Sum, are charged to 'Production contractual' over the period for which the site is coaling and are related to accounting periods on an output basis. Haulage to disposal point is charged under that profit and loss account heading, whilst the charges of contractors who operate the Executive's disposal points are charged under the heading 'Preparation contractual'. Appropriate provision is made in respect of the escalation relevant to each accounting period.

(iv) Provision is made during the coaling life of a site to cover the estimated costs to be incurred during the five year agricultural rehabilitation period, including the estimated escalation of those costs during that period. The item is charged under the heading 'Rehabilitation and compensation'.

(v) Management overheads and services are charged under those headings in the profit and loss account.

Other costs incurred by the Executive in the opencast mining activity, but not involving their main contractors, such as light and heat, wages of their operational staff, general rates in respect of coaling sites and disposal points, depreciation of NCB plant on sites and at disposal points, major maintenance, repair or reconstruction of Executive assets and so on are charged as appropriate to 'Other site and DP (disposal point) expenses', 'Depreciation' or 'Major revenue expenditure'. The heading 'Gross social costs', being related to redundancy and similar costs, has little materiality in the accounts of the Executive. The purchase of land for operational purposes is capitalised but provision is made under the heading 'Rehabilitation and compensation' for any anticipated or realised loss on disposal.

Staffing of NCB Industrial Relations and Staff Departments at end 1981–82

	National headquarters	Regional headquarters	Area headquarters	Headquarters establishments	Collieries	Totals
Industrial Relations Department						
Senior management	9	5	13	1	—	28
Management	40	74 (56)	196	10(a)	100	420 (402)
Clerical & Secretarial	23	443 (141)	146	15	—	627 (325)
All IR	72	522 (202)	355	26	100	1,075 (755)
Staff Department						
Senior management	16	1	10	3	—	(30)
Management	62	21	71	8	—	(162)
Clerical & Secretarial	39	39	107	10	—	(195)
All Staff Department	117	61	188	21	—	(387)
IR + Staff Department						
Senior management	25	6	23	4	—	58
Management	102	95 (77)	267	18	100	582 (564)
Clerical & Secretarial	62	482 (180)	253	25	—	822 (520)
All IR and Staff Department	189	583 (263)	543	47	100	1,462 (1,142)

Source: MMC from NCB information.

(a) Including 2 'scientific' staff.

Note: The figures in brackets refer to the relevant staffing levels after discounting the people doing 'agency' work on the basis described in the footnote to paragraph 12.3.

APPENDIX 12.2
(referred to in paragraph 12.12)

Disputes in coal mining and in all industries and services

Year	(A) No of disputes			(B) '000s man-days lost			(C) Man-days lost/'000 emp		Financial Year	(D) Coal lost %
	Coal	All	Coal/all %	Coal	All	Coal/all %	Coal	All		
Average 1947 to 1957	1,367	1,940	70·5	596	2,725	21·9	802	129		0·77
Average 1958 to 1968	1,050	2,370	44·3	334	3,403	9·8	578	148		0·70
1969	186	3,116	6·0	1,039	6,846	15·2	2,700	300	69/70	2·02
1970	160	3,906	4·1	1,090	10,980	9·9	3,050	475	70/71	2·26
1971	135	2,228	6·1	63	13,551	0·5	175	600	71/72	19·43
1972	224	2,497	9·0	10,798	23,909	45·2	32,750	1,100	72/73	0·50
1973	301	2,873	10·5	90	7,197	1·3	275	325	73/74	17·81
1974	186	2,922	6·4	5,625	14,750	38·1	18,775	647	74/75	0·36
1975	212	2,282	9·3	52	6,012	0·9	172	265	75/76	0·45
1976	276	2,016	13·7	70	3,284	2·1	235	146	76/77	1·01
1977	262	2,703	9·7	88	10,142	0·9	295	448	77/78	0·79
1978	338	2,471	13·7	195	9,405	2·1	660	413	78/79	1·39
1979	298	2,080	14·3	113	29,474	0·4	392	1,286	79/80	0·87
1980	302	1,330	22·7	152	11,964	1·3	532	531	80/81	1·32
1981	302	1,338	22·5	235	4,266	5·5	856	201	81/82	1·04

Sources: Department of Employment (A, B, C), the NCB (D).

Notes: Col A is disputes resulting in stoppages of work reported to Department of Employment or its predecessors: stoppages involving less than 10 men or lasting less than 1 day are excluded, except where total lost man-days exceeded 100.

Col B is man-days lost by participants in stoppages and by those at the same establishment laid off consequently: excluded are those lost due to lay-offs elsewhere.

Col C figures for 1969 to 1981 are DE published figures; pre-1969 they are MMC estimates, based on financial year figures for NCB total employees in coal mining and on DE figures for employees in employment at mid-year (all industries and services in Great Britain), together with the man-days lost figures from col B.

188

APPENDIX 12.3

(referred to in paragraph 12.12(c))

Causes of man-shifts lost, 1974–75 to 1981–82

	1974–75	1975–76	1976–77	1977–78	1978–79	1979–80	1980–81	1981–82
Dissatisfaction with allowances and bonuses	10,776	896	4,496	19,004	100,306	68,063	51,913	44,116
Refusal to accept reasonable alternative work	5,033	6,909	6,022	6,550	4,531	2,736	8,875	1,533
Sympathy with men dismissed, suspended or reprimanded	3,855	8,796	4,650	4,278	16,868	4,825	14,910	3,833
Refusal to perform work left over from previous shift	163	135	654	286	989	325	2,089	579
Terms & conditions of 5 day week agreement	1,554	1,379	1,492	5,508	1,237	183	341	6,119
Refusal to await repairs after m/c breakdown	263	236	377	263	47	87	62	94
Objection to or disputes about officials	10,544	2,472	30,971	7,034	633	3,879	4,581	1,218
Personnel or grading questions	1,115	550	52	1,857	91	2,587	5	768
Wages & price lists	5,410	5,204	3,996	15,348	4,304	4,009	4,624	3,550
Alleged bad working conditions	2,282	4,115	6,774	5,725	6,546	10,407	4,582	11,454
Methods of working and general organisation	7,825	7,068	10,095	9,512	9,232	16,431	12,309	22,493
Miscellaneous	7,948	2,543	10,436	7,532	9,733	23,914	87,867	6,927
Retaliatory disputes	6,915	13,255	9,105	9,353	16,602	10,310	14,093	20,514
Protest against closures, redundancies, or transfers	32	4	258	—	2,036	1,636	111,684	3,414
Disputes resulting from industrial action by officials	—	—	—	3,271	9,411	1,930	6,479	11,818
Totals	63,715	53,562	89,378	95,521	182,566	151,322	324,414	138,430

Source: The NCB.

The formal joint consultative machine (coal mining side only)

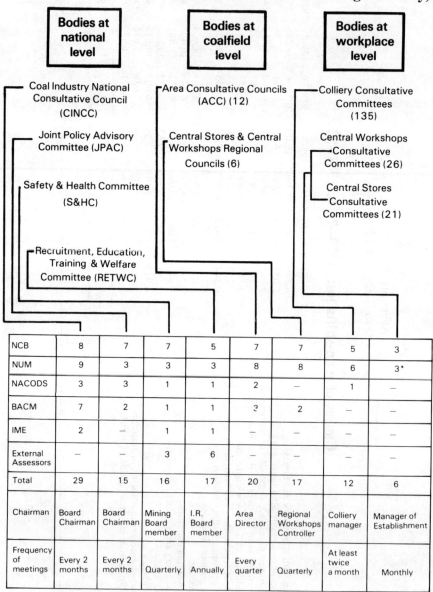

Bodies at national level			Bodies at coalfield level			Bodies at workplace level	
NCB	8	7	7	5	7	7	5	3
NUM	9	3	3	3	8	8	6	3*
NACODS	3	3	1	1	2	—	1	—
BACM	7	2	1	1	2	2	—	—
IME	2	—	1	1	—	—	—	—
External Assessors	—	—	3	6	—	—	—	—
Total	29	15	16	17	20	17	12	6
Chairman	Board Chairman	Board Chairman	Mining Board member	I.R. Board member	Area Director	Regional Workshops Controller	Colliery manager	Manager of Establishment
Frequency of meetings	Every 2 months	Every 2 months	Quarterly	Annually	Every quarter	Quarterly	At least twice a month	Monthly

*Plus up to 3 NUM Lodge Secretaries ex-officio.

Source: The NCB.

Colliery Review Procedure

The following is the text of a letter from the Directors General of Industrial Relations and Staff Departments to the NUM, NACODS and BACM, which sets out the purpose and the agreed procedure of the Colliery Review Procedure.

You will remember that, when the Board, the NUM, NACODS and BACM wrote jointly to Mr Boardman on 4 September, 1972 we said:

'We have agreed the principles of a new procedure for the joint review of colliery performance at Area level which we all consider of major importance. The proposition is that there will, as a routine, be a review by coalfields of the performance and future of all pits with Area representatives of the three Unions, in a continuing series of regular periodical meetings. The object will be to identify pits with particular problems and seek to resolve these in the most effective manner.

If, in spite of all efforts, certain pits still remain heavy losers, and due to exceptional circumstances closure seems inevitable, such closures will only take place after consultation with the Unions and having full regard to the interests of those affected (this aspect is referred to under the section relating to Government measures).'

The purpose of this letter is to suggest how the detailed arrangements might work.

You will recall that the previous position was that the arrangements for review of collieries were dealt with as part of the Consultative Committee procedures. On the occasions when a particular pit showed especially serious results, the colliery (and higher Union officials) were warned that the results were such as to put the future of the pit in jeopardy. Where the Board decided to close, the NUM had a right of appeal against that decision.

What we now suggest is a totally new procedure, in that there would be a systematic analysis of the results of all collieries in an Area (whatever their results) at least once every three months. This analysis would be made at meetings between the Area Director and Area representatives of the three Unions. The accent would be on discussing constructive ways of improving results. In the course of those discussions the Area Director would identify those collieries where special action was required, and would call for suggestions from the Area Union representatives. Attention would be given to getting even better results from pits which were doing well, as well as to the means of improving disappointing results. About three weeks later, this meeting would reconvene, and concentrate on key points identified in the earlier discussions. Colliery representatives could be invited to attend the meeting if a particular colliery was being specially considered. Area representatives of the Unions might earlier have visited the particular colliery. The old concept of 'jeopardy' would disappear.

Whilst the purpose of these meetings is to improve results, and secure the maximum efficiency and optimum future for the industry and those who work in it, we all recognised that some pits would have to close, either through exhaustion or because of heavy losses or changing markets, and the Area Director at one of the Review Procedure meetings would have to explain that he could not justify keeping the colliery open. He would present to the Unions' representatives a written statement of the reason for his decision together with his detailed proposals for any redundancies which arose as a result. Copies of this statement would also be sent to the Area Offices of the Unions concerned.

The Board would hope that in such cases agreement would be reached locally that the colliery could not continue in production, and the Unions nationally would be informed of the decision. If, however, no agreement could be reached locally, the Area Director would report this to the Board. If the Board, from a national stand-point, could see no suitable justification to keep a colliery open, they would inform national Unions. The Unions would have the opportunity to make a technical inspection and study market prospects.

There would be provision for a national meeting (within a month of the notification by the Board to the national Unions) if the Unions so desire. After this the Board, as managers, would decide whether the colliery must close. In such circumstances they would normally give four months' notice to the Unions.

Thus where an Area Director cannot justify continued operation, the procedure available to the Union would be as follows:

	Time from start
(1) The Area Director has one of his Colliery Review Procedure Meetings with Area Unions.	—
(2) Meeting reconvened. Special attention given to the particular colliery.	3 weeks
(3) Area Director reports to the National Board he cannot justify continued operation.	1 month
(4) The National Board (if appropriate) tell the National Unions they cannot see how they could justify continued operation.	—
(5) If the Unions do not agree, they may make a technical inspection.	—
(6) The Unions may ask for a national appeal meeting.	2 months
(7) The National Coal Board consider points made at appeal meeting, decide whether to close and, if so, announce it will take place in four months' time.	$2\frac{1}{2}$ months
(8) Colliery closes; individual notices terminate.	$6\frac{1}{2}$ months

This new review procedure will need to fit into our existing local consultative procedures. Local practices vary slightly, however, and the way in which they fit together may best be left for local discussion between Area Directors and the Area officials of the Unions concerned.

National Coal Board
November 1972

(referred to in paragraphs 13.12, 13.15 and 13.40)

Operation of the incentive scheme

1. Following is a description of how the details of an installation agreement are applied to determine the level of incentive pay at a hypothetical coal face. The amount payable for standard performance is £6 per shift as laid down nationally. The ways in which the various calculations are applied to the figures in order to determine incentive pay are the same in all the Area agreements:

    (a) *Agreed standards* (hypothetical example)

        standard task per shift=320 metres
        standard manning   = 20 men
        depth of strip   = 60 centimetres

    (b) *Calculations based on standards* (using the example above)

        (i) Standard task per man-shift $=\dfrac{\text{standard task per shift}}{\text{manning}}$

$$=\frac{320}{20}=16 \text{ metres}$$

This means that if the face team averaged 16 metres of coal cut per man-shift at the standard depth of cut during a week, each team member would get £6 incentive pay for each shift he worked (subject to a calculation to be applied if overtime is worked—see paragraph 6 below).

        (ii) Basic task per man-shift=75 per cent of standard task
$$=0{\cdot}75 \times 16 \text{ metres}$$
$$=12 \text{ metres}$$

This means that if performance averages 12 metres per man-shift or below, no incentive pay would have been earned, except subject to fall-back pay arrangements (see paragraph 7).

        (iii) Incentive rate per metre per shift

$$=\frac{\text{the amount payable for standard performance}}{\text{the difference between standard and basic tasks}}$$

$$=\frac{£6}{16-12}=£6 \div 4=£1{\cdot}50$$

This means that the incentive pay per man-shift worked goes up by £1·50 for each metre cut over the basic of 12 metres per man-shift, so that if the performance over a week averages 13 metres per man-shift then incentive pay is £1·50 per man-shift, if performance averages 14 metres, then incentive pay is £3·00 per man-shift and so on, reaching £6·00 at the 16 metre standard (as noted in (i) above) £7·50 at 17 metres, £9·00 at 18 metres: there is no upper limit.

    (c) *Level of incentive pay*
    Suppose there were no complications and the face achieved 1,750 metres in five normal weekday shifts, with full manning, no major

interruptions to production and the specified depth of strip cut, then the incentive pay per man for the week would be calculated as follows:

Incentive pay = (recorded performance—basic task)
multiplied by the incentive rate per metre

$$= \left(\frac{1{,}750}{100 \text{ man-shifts}} - 12 \text{ per man-shift}\right) \times £1{\cdot}50$$

$$= £8{\cdot}25 \text{ per shift}$$

$$= £41{\cdot}25 \text{ per five-shift week per man.}$$

This calculation illustrates a general feature of the scheme, that there is a disproportionate relationship between performance relative to standard and incentive pay relative to the standard amount. Here a performance which was 9·375 per cent above the standard set resulted in incentive pay which was 37·5 per cent above the standard amount. In general, for a performance X per cent above standard at standard manning with no major interruptions, incentive pay per man-shift is 4X per cent above the standard £6.

2. There are a number of factors which lead to complications in the way incentive earnings are derived from the measured performance levels; variation from standard depth of strip, variation from standard manning, interruptions to production, overtime working and fall-back pay are the main factors involved.

3. An improvement over standard for the depth of strip cut is dealt with by applying a proportionate correction factor to the recorded performance level. In the example in paragraph 1(a) the standard depth of cut was agreed at 60 centimetres: if the actual depth of cut averaged, say, 63 centimetres then the recorded performance level would be multiplied by a factor of $\frac{63}{60}$, so that the incentive pay calculation at paragraph 1(c) would come out as:

$$\left(\frac{1{,}750 \times \frac{63}{60}}{100} - 12\right) \times £1{\cdot}50$$

$$= £9{\cdot}5625 \text{ per shift or } £47{\cdot}8125 \text{ per five-shift week per man.}$$

Thus a 5 per cent increase in depth of cut (and hence tonnage) resulted in a 16 per cent increase in incentive pay compared with that for the performance in the example at standard depth of cut. A less than standard depth of cut would cause a reduction in the recorded performance levels, and hence earnings, to the extent of any excess shortfall over 5 per cent, eg suppose the actual depth of cut was 57 centimetres against a standard of 60 centimetres, then the shortfall is only 5 per cent and would be tolerated. If, however, the depth of cut were 56 centimetres then an adjustment of 1 centimetre would be applied

$$\left(\frac{1{,}750 \times \frac{59}{60}}{100} - 12\right) \times £1{\cdot}50$$

$$= £7{\cdot}8125 \text{ per shift or } £39{\cdot}0625 \text{ per five-shift week per man,}$$

ie only 5·3 per cent less incentive pay for a 6·7 per cent shortfall in depth of cut.

4. Variation from standard manning acts so as to raise per capita incentive earnings in the case of undermanning or depress them in the case of overmanning, but offset to the extent that the performance level might itself alter in relation to the level of manning. Suppose in the example in paragraph 1 actual manning was one man light throughout the working week but performance was also down in the same proportion, then the recorded performance would be $\frac{19}{20}$ of 1,750 metres for (19×5) man-shifts worked. The incentive earnings would then be:

$$\left(\frac{1,750 \times \frac{19}{20}}{95} - 12 \right) \times £1 \cdot 50$$

=£8·25 per shift
=£41·25 per five-shift week per man present,
   ie no effect on earnings.

However, if the light team were able to achieve the same performance as a standard team (either because the agreed standard was excessive or because of some redeployment of men so as to have in effect a full production team despite its being recorded as light) then there is a pronounced effect on earnings, eg

$$\left(\frac{1,750}{95} - 12 \right) \times £1 \cdot 50$$

=£9·63 per shift
=£48·16 per five-shift week per man,
   being 16·7 per cent increase in earnings.

It should be noted, however, that this effect is exaggerated to the extent that the light team achieves an above standard overall performance. If a team one light achieved the standard task of 1,600 metres, then incentive earnings would be:

$$\left(\frac{1,600}{95} - 12 \right) \times £1 \cdot 50$$

=£7·2632 per shift
=£36·3158 per five-shift week per man.

In this case performance per man-shift would be 16·842105 metres, or approximately 5·3 per cent above standard, and per capita earnings would be the same as if a full team had worked at 5·3 per cent above standard.

5. Interruptions to production lasting 20 minutes or more and due to factors agreed to be beyond the control of the face team result in notional additions to the recorded performance at the basic task rate, according to a formula:

Added metres=basic task for man-shift× no. of men present×
$$\frac{\text{minutes of interruption}}{\text{minutes of machine available time}}$$

where the machine available time is a figure derived from the original method study and incorporated in the installation agreement, being that portion of the shift which could be devoted to coal cutting as distinct from travelling time, meal breaks, etc. So, for example, if the machine available time on the hypothetical face were 300 minutes per shift and an interruption of 30 minutes occurred in one shift during the week, then, assuming a proportionate (ie 10 per cent) reduction in performance in the interrupted shift, the effect on earnings might be as follows:

recorded performance for the week=1,715 (ie four shifts averaging 350 metres and one at 315 having lost 10 per cent of production time)

added metres for the interruption, at the basic task rate

$$=12\times20\times\frac{30}{300}=24$$

payment would be on the basis of (1,715+24) metres=1,739 metres

Incentive earnings would be:

$$\left(\frac{1,739}{100}-12\right)\quad\times£1\cdot50$$

=£8·085 per man-shift

=£40·425 per five-shift week per man, ie a 2 per cent loss of earnings corresponding to a 2 per cent loss of total production.

6. Working of a face in recorded overtime at the weekend results in an adjustment in performance figures which appear to have a neutral effect on earnings for the face team but distributes the gains equally according to the weekday shifts worked. This is because the recorded performance is adjusted downwards by a figure made up by multiplying the number of overtime man-shifts worked by the basic task rate, whilst the incentive pay calculation (paragraph 1(c)) uses as the divisor only the number of week-day shifts worked. For example, suppose that the hypothetical face was worked for one weekend shift in addition to five weekday shifts and achieved a proportionate 20 per cent increase in overall performance:

recorded performance   =2,100 metres (ie the 1,750 suggested in paragraph 1(c) plus 20 per cent)

overtime working   =20 man-shifts

deduction for overtime working at the basic rate
   =20×12 metres−240 metres

adjusted performance   =2,100−240 metres
   =1,860 metres

incentive pay $=\left(\frac{1,860}{100}-12\right)\quad\times£1\cdot50$

=£9·90 per shift

=£49·50 per five-shift week per man

This is the same as if the adjustment had not been made, the divisor of man-shifts had been all shifts worked and the per shift incentive pay multiplied by six instead of five to get the weekly payment.

7. The adjustment for fall-back pay is based on the agreement that any installation earning less than 65 per cent of the average for all installations in the colliery will have incentive pay brought up to that level. To take a simple example, suppose a colliery had only two faces, one earning £38 per man-week incentive pay, the other earning £15. The colliery average

196

(assuming that the same number of shifts were worked at each installation) would be:

$$£\frac{38+15}{2}=£26\cdot50; \text{ of which } 65\% \text{ is } £17\cdot23$$

and the men at the low earning face would be paid £17·23 incentive pay for the week instead of £15, or proportionately per shift worked. If there were a different number of shifts worked at each installation, the colliery average would be worked out on a weighted basis, using the number of shifts as weights.

(referred to in paragraph 13.43)

Distribution of performance levels against agreed standards at 557 coal faces and incentive earnings before adjustments [W/E 27/3/82]

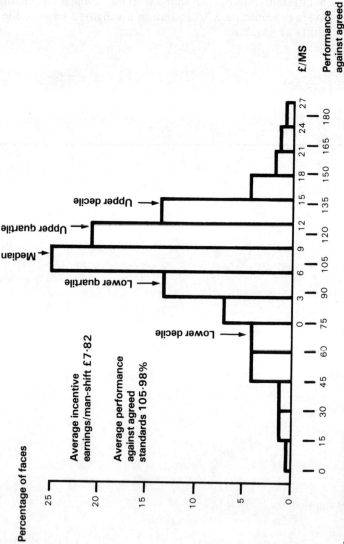

Source: MMC from NCB information.

(referred to in paragraph 13.43)

Distribution of performance levels against agreed standards at 526 drivages and incentive earnings before adjustments [W/E 27/3/82]

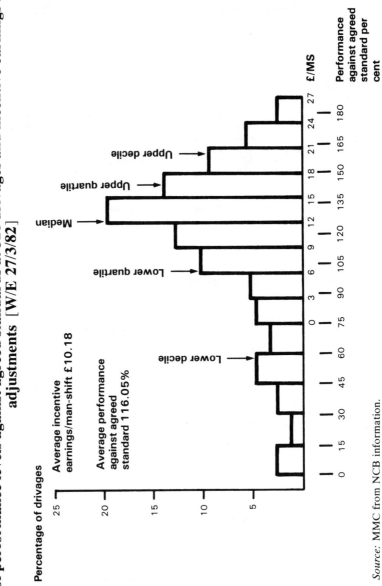

Source: MMC from NCB information.

(referred to in paragraph 14.42)

NCB remuneration package for non-industrial staff

Staff in receipt 1981–82

		Numbers	Amount £ p a
Bonus at 100%	Colliery line management and engineers		1,850
50%	Colliery surveyors, safety engineers, others with substantial underground working	All non-industrials	875
40%	All other clerical and managerial up to and including grade SG8		700
London allowance Inner: adults	All staff within 4 miles of Charing Cross	All	895
juveniles		London staff	645
Outer: adults	All staff outside inner area up to boundary		585
juveniles	of metropolitan police area		425
Colliery allowance At £1,040	Colliery and plant managerial staff in defined categories not eligible for attendance payments but who are likely to be	3,492	876
At £780	called on to make authorised attendances		
At £520	at weekends and on holidays for which time off in lieu is not possible: the amount depends on grade		
Attendance allowance	Managerial staff up to grade M2 and operations engineers up to M3 not eligible for colliery/plant allowance but actually called out to make additional attendances: payment depends on number of attendances	1,000	740
Underground allowance	Area staff with regular underground duties	200	250
Overtime	All clerical staff for overtime over ½hr on basic daily hours	5,744	895
Responsibility allowance	CO4 with supervisory responsibilities	833	145
Night allowance	All clerical staff for hours worked between 8.00 pm and 8.00 am	4,282	82
Travel-to-work costs Over £1·62 per week	All clerical staff	6,258	202
Over £1·90 per week	All managerial and SG	10,463	294

		Numbers	Amount £ p a
Concessionary fuel	Householders stationed in coalfields: managerial	13,000	390
	clerical	8,300	275
Cars	Managers down to SG5, others with regular travelling duties		

Holidays
  23 days   for trainee and junior grades
  25 days   for all other non-industrial staff
                   plus 8 statutory holidays and 4 extra days

Sick pay
  Full salary   for 6 months, thereafter half salary for 6 months

Pensions
  Individual   5% females   less 1% if joined
  contributions at 6% males   scheme before 1964

  Pension is up to 40/80ths of salary in last year or, if better, any of last five years or best three of last ten years, as increased by the rise in the RPI.

Source: The NCB.

Comparison of the NCB clerical salaries and those shown in Department of Employment New Earnings Survey for all industries and services

(A) NCB clerical grades: annual cost at July 1981

	£
Basic salaries	46,917,138
Overtime	5,048,655
Responsibility allowances	126,137
Incentive bonus	6,585,147
Night allowance	347,958
London allowance	247,550
Total salaries	59,272,585
Travel allowance	1,116,621
Concessionary fuel (est)	1,674,735
Total remuneration	62,063,941

Average for 9,715 clerical staff in grades SCO–CO4

	£
Basic salary	4,829
Basic + bonus	5,507
Total salary	6,101
Total remuneration	6,388

Source: The NCB.

(B) NES figures for clerks' earnings at April 1981

(i) Earnings of full-time clerical and related adult men (excl absentees) number in sample: 7,060

Total weekly earnings	Overtime	PBR[1] etc	Shift etc premia	All other pay
£119·4	£8·9	£2·1	£2·6	£105·7

(ii) Earnings of full-time clerical and related adult women (excl absentees) number in sample: 16,436

Total weekly earnings	Overtime	PBR[1] etc	Shift etc premia	All other pay
£84·7	£1·2	£0·9	£0·3	£82·3

(iii) Weighted average of the above number in sample: 23,496

Total weekly earnings	Overtime	PBR[1] etc	Shift etc premia	All other pay
£95·12	£3·51	£1·26	£0·99	£89·33

(iv) Weighted average of the above in proportion 61 per cent male/39 per cent female, as in NCB workforce

Total weekly earnings	Overtime	PBR[1] etc	Shift etc premia	All other pay
£105·9	£5·9	£1·6	£1·7	£96·6

Source: MMC from NES 1981 and NCB information.

[1]PBR=Payment by results.

(C) Comparison of NES and NCB figures

NCB salaries etc at A above may be compared with annualised NES figures on the basis of NES male/female weighting (B(iii) above) or NCB weighting (B(iv) above) as follows:

	£	Coal as % of NES on each basis
Basic salary NCB	4,829	
All other pay NES (NES weightings)	4,645	104
,, ,, ,, ,, (NCB weightings)	5,023	96
Basic + bonus NCB	5,507	
Basic + PBR[1] etc NES (NES weightings)	4,711	117
,, ,, ,, (NCB weightings)	5,106	108
Total salary NCB	6,101	
Total salary NES (NES weightings)	4,946	123
,, ,, ,, (NCB weightings)	5,507	111
Total remuneration NCB	6,388	has no NES equivalent

Source: MMC from NES and NCB information.

[1]PBR=Payment by results.

APPENDIX 16.1
(referred to in paragraph 16.1)

Headquarters Purchasing and Stores Department

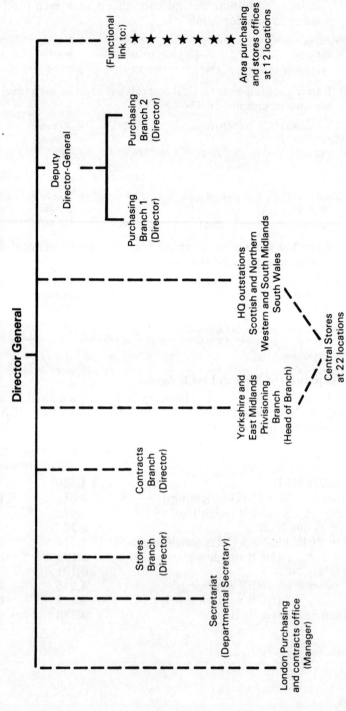

December 1981

Source: The NCB.

Summary of main purchasing and stock control functions by organisation level

Headquarters P & S

Setting up of national contracts.

Stock control and ordering of headquarter designated items: eg mining timber, arches, conveyor belting, line pans, etc.

Plant pool purchases.

Headquarters outstation

Stock control and ordering of items for Central Stores and colliery stocks.

Purchasing of stock items not on national contracts and not controlled by headquarters; direct purchasing for Central Workshops and other non-Area activities.

The management of Central Stores.

Area P & S

All direct purchasing of non-stock items required by collieries; involves ordering against national contracts and purchasing of non-contract items.

Central Stores

Central stockholding points serving collieries and workshops. Typically stockholding rationalised on regional basis around a number of central stores.

No routine stock control or purchasing responsibilities.

Colliery Stores

No Central Stores items held at colliery level other than imprest stock replenished on average fortnightly through travelling requisitions.

Other items called up from Central Stores as required by users.

Non-Central Stores stock (ie 'colliery inventory') is subject to direct headquarters outstation stock control.

Direct purchases through Area are not held in stock.

Increase in the NCB's average purchase price index by purchase category 1973 to 1981

Increase in the average purchase price index (by classification) over average 1973–74 level

Classification	Description	1973 –74	1974 –75	1975 –76	1976 –77	1977 –78	1978 –79	1979 –80	1980 –81	1981 –82
01	Arches and accessories.	100	154·4	193·5	261·1	302·8	328·6	353·8	365·8	376·0
02A	Props and bars.	100	130·8	169·0	192·4	223·1	257·1	307·7	350·9	377·2
02B	Powered roof supports and spares.	100	115·5	137·2	152·7	178·7	202·5	222·4	245·9	262·7
03	Straight joists and sections.	100	151·6	190·8	239·4	279·9	303·6	321·7	328·9	338·0
04	Rail tube, plate and other steel sections.	100	157·2	183·9	225·3	247·9	261·3	273·5	287·7	287·4
05	Mining timber.	100	137·2	144·5	153·0	173·6	194·9	222·9	264·3	264·0
06	Other timber.	100	129·8	129·8	145·3	170·8	171·5	189·3	202·0	203·0
07	Building requisites.	100	134·9	174·2	204·0	243·9	266·7	307·8	359·9	392·3
08	Oils and greases.	100	180·8	212·3	266·6	307·9	304·7	432·3	542·6	604·1
09	Explosives.	100	118·0	151·0	176·4	198·7	218·9	246·9	306·4	372·1
10	Conveyor belting and accessories.	100	154·0	180·0	211·8	250·9	272·5	300·1	343·1	346·0
11	Wire ropes and accessories.	100	129·4	188·2	235·1	274·8	305·8	358·7	408·1	435·5
12	Electrical equipment, material, cable and wire.	100	116·9	144·3	169·2	188·1	204·8	231·4	275·1	300·6
13	Chemicals, hose, bolts and nuts, packings, tools, protective accessories and other general materials and stores.	100	124·4	148·8	167·7	202·2	220·4	242·2	268·8	277·3
14	Coal-face, roadway and stowing machinery.	100	121·4	154·7	181·3	207·4	229·5	266·3	301·9	323·2
15	Spares for coal-face, roadway and stowing machinery and materials handling equipment.	100	121·3	154·7	181·3	206·3	237·8	276·4	315·7	344·8
16	Linepans and coal-cutting tools. Underground locos and haulage pumps. All items of surface plant and equipment.	100	127·7	172·3	211·8	255·2	281·1	318·3	376·5	419·6
17	Associated spares for classification 16.	100	119·8	162·1	184·6	211·5	234·1	259·5	290·3	308·5
18	Stationery and office equipment.	100	132·6	146·2	161·6	183·2	175·5	195·0	221·4	241·9
	Total	100	129·3	158·9	186·5	214·4	236·7	266·3	301·5	322·3
	Wholesale price index, mechanical engineering output.	100	126·4	158·1	184·6	213·4	237·4	268·0	301·5	325·1

Source: The NCB.

Outstation organisation: Yorks and East Midlands

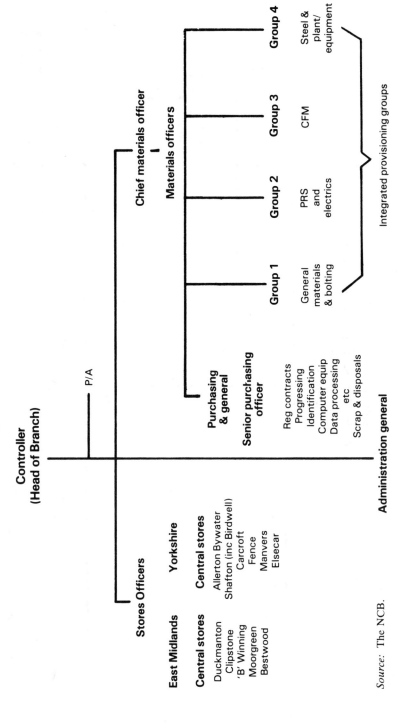

Source: The NCB.

207

APPENDIX 16.5
(referred to in paragraph 16.55)
Central stores: Typical organisation

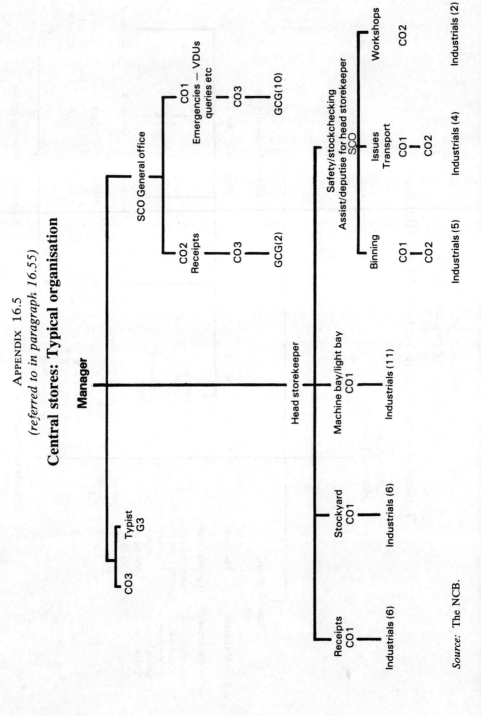

Source: The NCB.

208

Summary of stock control methods

Stock control methods	*Main categories of items covered*
Cyclic review or distribution (manual or computerised) through HQ	Arches, steel tube, rail joists FR conveyor belting Mining timber Hose High value/critical Coal-face machinery spares
Materials generally handled by local (outstation) cyclic review or similar methods	Cable Renovated items Some general stores
Order point systems	General stores Engineering materials
Order point + kitting up procedures	Spares for coal-face machinery, including powered supports
Special arrangements including call off from standing orders, depletion stocks, etc	Oils & greases Building materials
Standby and other stocks where user reference often necessary	Winder spares Coal preparation plant spares

Source: MMC.

APPENDIX 16.7
(referred to in paragraph 16.89)

Purchasing and Stores at NCB Area levels

(From 1981 Census)

Area		1973	1974	1975	1976	1977	1978	1979	1980	1981
Scotland	General		1	1	1	1	1	1	1	1
	Management and Technical	11	9	8	8	8	9	9	9	9
	Clerical	26	26	31	29	28	28	26	25	25
North East	General			2	2	1	1	1	1	1
	Management and Technical	9	7	12	12	12	12	11	8	8
	Clerical	22	19	24	24	23	21	20	20	21
North Yorkshire	General		1	1	1	1	1	1	1	1
	Management and Technical	3	6	9	10	12	13	13	12	13
	Clerical	9	10	10	13	14	15	15	15	16
Doncaster	General	1	1	1	1	1	1	1	1	1
	Management and Technical	4	6	8	10	11	11	14	14	13
	Clerical	12	13	14	15	15	15	17	18	19
Barnsley	General		1	1	1	1	1	1	1	1
	Management and Technical	4	15	7	7	10	9	11	11	11
	Clerical	9	6	17	21	21	24	27	27	29
South Yorkshire	General			1	1	1	1	1	1	—
	Management and Technical	5	6	6	8	8	8	8	9	9
	Clerical	12	13	16	16	14	14	16	15	17
North Derbyshire	General		1	1	1	1	1	1	1	1
	Management and Technical	7	7	7	7	7	7	7	7	7
	Clerical	12	15	17	13	13	13	13	13	13
North Notts	General		1	1	1	1	1	1	1	1
	Management and Technical	5	7	7	8	8	8	8	8	8
	Clerical	12	13	17	15	18	19	20	19	19
South Notts	General		1	1	1	1	1	1	1	1
	Management and Technical	4	4	6	7	7	8	8	7	10
	Clerical	12	16	16	18	19	17	17	17	16
South Midlands	General		1	1	1	1	1	1	1	1
	Management and Technical	11	6	8	9	10	10	8	9	10
	Clerical	26	12	12	15	21	21	25	24	21
Western	General		1	1	1	1	1	1	1	1
	Management and Technical	9	9	9	11	11	11	11	11	11
	Clerical	23	23	17	19	19	18	16	16	16
South Wales	General		1	1	2	1	1	1	1	1
	Management and Technical	29	22	23	23	14	15	15	15	14
	Clerical	65	70	72	77	36	37	35	33	31
		342	349	385	409	371	375	382	374	367

Source: The NCB.

Purchasing & Stores Department
(central revenue expenditure (£'000))

HQ		1980–81			1981–82 (Part year)	
	Budget	Actual	% Spent	Budget for year	Actual 9 months to December	% Spent
Salaries and related expenses	3,955	3,966	100·3	4,464	3,216	72·0
Compower charges	4,306	4,024	93·5	4,553	3,267	71·8
Other expenses	424	328	77·4	480	269	56·0
Gross expenditure	8,685	8,318	95·8	9,497	6,752	71·1
Outstations						
Salaries & related expenses	2,938	2,941	100·1	3,024	2,233	73·8
Other expenses	78	71	91·0	89	62	69·7
Gross expenditure	3,016	3,012	99·9	3,113	2,295	73·7
Central stores						
Salaries and related expenses	3,260	3,110	95·4	3,317	2,421	73·0
Wages and wages charges	4,646	4,787	103·0	5,111	3,685	72·1
Other expenses	5,290	5,387	101·8	5,940	4,169	70·2
Gross expenditure	13,196	13,284	100·7	14,368	10,275	71·5
Print units						
Salaries and related expenses	414	412	99·5	417	306	73·4
Wages and wages charges	16	16	100·0	18	15	83·3
Other expenses	945	796	84·2	1,017	531	52·2
Gross expenditure	1,375	1,224	89·0	1,452	852	58·7
Grand total						
Salaries and related expenses	10,567	10,429	98·7	11,222	8,176	72·9
Wages and wages charges	4,662	4,803	103·0	5,129	3,700	72·1
Compower charges	4,306	4,024	93·5	4,553	3,267	71·8
Other expenses	6,737	6,582	97·7	7,526	5,031	66·8
Gross expenditure	26,272	25,838	98·3	28,430	20,174	71·0

	Budget Mar 81	Actual Mar 81	+/—	Budget Mar 82	Acutal Mar 82	+/—
Staff in post						
HQ	443	449	+6	430	429	−1
Outstations	384	373	−11	348	351	+3
Central stores	487	466	−21	473	439	−34
Print units	60	56	−4	58	57	−1
Total	1,374	1,344	−30	1,309	1,276	−33
Decrease on 1980–81				65	68	

Source: The NCB.

National Coal Board
Hobart House, Grosvenor Place, London SW1X 7AE
Telex: 882161 (CBHOB G)
Station Code HOB

Staff Department

December 1981

Gifts and Favours and Hospitality

I am writing to you and to all the Board's staff to draw attention to the Board's rules about the acceptance of gifts, favours and hospitality. These rules apply at all times and are particularly relevant during the Christmas season. The Board intend that they will be interpreted strictly.

General Principle

The Board expect from their staff the highest standards of integrity and personal conduct. Staff must not misuse their position with the Board for personal advantage. Staff must have in mind at all times the need to avoid any suspicion that in their capacity as employees of the Board they may be influenced by any gift or consideration to show favour or disfavour to any individual or organisation.

Gifts and Favours

Staff must decline gifts and favours from any individual, firm or company which does or might do business with the Board, where the gift or favour is offered to them, or may reasonably appear to be so offered, in their capacity as employees of the Board; and this applies whether the gift or favour is offered at the place of work or elsewhere. For this purpose 'favour' includes any financial or other advantage, whether tangible or intangible, except hospitality and entertainment, which is dealt with separately below. Examples of favours are offers of goods or services either free or at a discount (otherwise than through a discount scheme recognised by the Board); payment of expenses (for instance, expenses in connection with conferences at home or overseas); and the provision of facilities, such as membership of clubs.

The only exception to this rule comprises gifts of trade advertisement calendars, diaries, and similar items of trivial value: provided that such items are for use on Board premises and are plainly advertisements, they may be accepted.

If a gift is received which, under the rule set out above, must be declined, the recipient must return it to the sender explaining that this is being done on the Board's instructions; and the recipient must inform an appropriate superior official of what has taken place. If any member of the staff is in doubt about whether to accept a gift or favour, or about the effect of the rule, he must consult an appropriate superior official and act in accordance with his instructions. In all cases covered by this paragraph the superior official must make a written record which must be permanently retained.

Hospitality and Entertainment

Staff must decline hospitality or entertainment if it is of such a nature that the Board cannot reciprocate it, or are not likely to wish to do so; or if it is on a scale significantly more generous than anything which the Board would be likely to provide in return. Frequent offers of hospitality from the same source must be declined. Other forms of entertainment, including, for example, invitations to manufacturers' exhibitions, and subsidised visits to conferences, may be accepted only when they are for purposes in the Board's business interest and when prior authorisation of an appropriate superior official has been obtained—except where this is impracticable. In any event the circumstances of an acceptance must be fully documented and a permanent record must be retained.

Special Cases

The Board recognise that occasions may arise, especially in countries over-seas where conditions differ from our own, where a refusal of a gift, favour, hospitality or entertainment in accordance with the foregoing rules may offend the giver. In such circumstances members of staff must, wherever practicable, consult an appropriate superior official beforehand and act in accordance with his instructions. If this is not practicable (for instance, in the course of overseas visits where communication is difficult) staff must keep in mind the general principle at the beginning of this letter and exercise discretion. Wherever a member of staff accepts a gift, favour, hospitality or entertainment in these special circumstances, he must inform an appropriate superior official as soon as practicable. He must also record fully the acceptance and the circumstances and send the record to the appropriate Staff Manager. If the acceptance is of a gift, the Board may require him to hand it over to them.

Families and Friends

The rules set out above apply equally to gifts, favours, hospitality and entertainment provided or offered, with the knowledge of a member of the staff and by virtue of his employment with the Board, to members of his family or to his friends.

Yours sincerely

P. W. Glover
Director-General of Staff

Printed for Her Majesty's Stationery Office by McCorquodale Printers Ltd.,
HM 1856 Dd 163910 C20 6/83